The IDEATE Method

Our expectation: After *completing* this entire workbook by following the
principles of the IDEATE method, you will generate 100 ideas.
You need at least 100 ideas to get to a high-potential entrepreneurial opportunity.

Sara Miller McCune founded SAGE Publishing in 1965 to support
the dissemination of usable knowledge and educate a global
community. SAGE publishes more than 1000 journals and over
800 new books each year, spanning a wide range of subject areas.
Our growing selection of library products includes archives, data,
case studies and video. SAGE remains majority owned by our
founder and after her lifetime will become owned by a charitable
trust that secures the company's continued independence.

Los Angeles | London | New Delhi | Singapore | Washington DC | Melbourne

The IDEATE Method

Identifying High-Potential Entrepreneurial Ideas

Dan Cohen
Wake Forest University

Greg Pool
Wake Forest University

Heidi Neck
Babson College

Los Angeles | London | New Delhi
Singapore | Washington DC | Melbourne

FOR INFORMATION:

SAGE Publications, Inc.
2455 Teller Road
Thousand Oaks, California 91320
E-mail: order@sagepub.com

SAGE Publications Ltd.
1 Oliver's Yard
55 City Road
London, EC1Y 1SP
United Kingdom

SAGE Publications India Pvt. Ltd.
B 1/I 1 Mohan Cooperative Industrial Area
Mathura Road, New Delhi 110 044
India

SAGE Publications Asia-Pacific Pte. Ltd.
18 Cross Street #10-10/11/12
China Square Central
Singapore 048423

Printed in the United States of America

Library of Congress Cataloging-in-Publication Data

Names: Cohen, Dan, author. | Pool, Greg, author. | Neck, Heidi, author.

Title: The IDEATE method: Identifying high-potential entrepreneurial ideas / Dan Cohen, Wake Forest University, Greg Pool, Wake Forest University, Heidi Neck, Babson College.

Description: Los Angeles : SAGE, [2021] | Includes bibliographical references.

Identifiers: LCCN 2019034578 | ISBN 978-1-5443-9324-7 (paperback) | ISBN 978-1-5443-9325-4 (epub) | ISBN 978-1-5443-9326-1 (epub)

Subjects: LCSH: New products. | Creative ability in business. | New business enterprises. | Entrepreneurship.

Classification: LCC HF5415.153.C624 2021 | DDC 658.4/063—dc23

LC record available at https://lccn.loc.gov/2019034578

This book is printed on acid-free paper.

Acquisitions Editor: Maggie Stanley
Editorial Assistant: Janeane Calderon
Production Editor: Rebecca Lee
Copy Editor: Diana Breti
Typesetter: Cenveo Publisher Services
Proofreader: Annie Lubinsky
Cover Designer: Ginkhan Siam
Marketing Manager: Sarah Panella

20 21 22 23 24 10 9 8 7 6 5 4 3 2 1

BRIEF CONTENTS

DETAILED CONTENTS

PREFACE

The seeds of the IDEATE framework germinated at Cornell University, where Dan Cohen was the founding director of eLab—Cornell's startup accelerator. Cohen noticed that many of the startups that got traction in eLab originated in his "Foundations of Entrepreneurship" course. When making conference presentations about eLab, Cohen heard many professors complain that their students lacked the ability to come up with valuable entrepreneurial ideas. This certainly wasn't a problem Cohen had; his students were quite capable of spotting, evaluating, and selecting valuable ideas and, in fact, were doing so regularly. Based on feedback from his fellow professors, however, he realized his experience was not the norm. This motivated Cohen to formalize his approach to teaching ideation so the model could be replicated and taught in other settings—thus, the birth of a framework he named IDEATE (Identify, Discover, Enhance, Anticipate, Target, Evaluate).

In 2015, Cohen joined the faculty at Wake Forest University, where he began working closely with Greg Pool, a serial entrepreneur who had recently transitioned to a faculty appointment teaching entrepreneurship. Together, they refined the IDEATE framework into a detailed method and conducted an experiment to validate its efficacy.

Deciding to get the method published in order to reach a broader audience, Cohen and Pool reached out to Heidi Neck, author of a leading entrepreneurship textbook. Cohen and Pool were already using her textbook, *Entrepreneurship: The Practice and Mindset*, in their classes and were excited about the work she was producing, so they asked if she would be willing to contribute her experience and knowledge to the effort. Her expertise in entrepreneurship education helped create the pedagogical structure necessary to ensure students could easily navigate the method while also maximizing their learning and ability to replicate the method in the future.

Cohen, Pool, and Neck want to reverse a disturbing trend: Entrepreneurial activity is declining among people under the age of 30. Although there are many possible causes for this decline, we believe that one of the causes is that inexperienced entrepreneurs have more difficulty than those with experience in spotting, evaluating, and selecting *high-potential* entrepreneurial ideas that can gain market acceptance. This fact motivated us to bring the IDEATE method to a wider audience. We are passionate about entrepreneurship education and believe in this method. Using IDEATE has been empirically proven to help students generate higher potential ideas than conventional methods.

ACKNOWLEDGMENTS

The authors and SAGE would like to thank the following instructors who participated in reviews:

John Callister, Cornell University

Jason D'Mello, Loyola Marymount University

Drew Hession-Kunz, Boston College

Mary Goebel-Lundholm, Peru State College

Dale Jasinski, Quinnipiac University

Lori Long, Baldwin Wallace University

Vincent Mangum, Atlanta Metropolitan State College

Gary Minkoff, Rutgers University

Charles Murnieks, Oregon State University

Jesse Pipes, Appalachian State University

Mark T. Schenkel, Belmont University

Jeffrey D. Stone, California State University, Channel Islands

ABOUT THE AUTHORS

Dan Cohen, PhD, is the John C. Whitaker Executive Director and Professor of Practice at the Center for Entrepreneurship at Wake Forest University. Over the course of his career, he has taught entrepreneurship and strategy at the undergraduate, graduate, and executive levels. Since coming to Wake Forest University in 2015, he has cofounded Startup Lab with Greg Pool and completely revamped all aspects of the Center for Entrepreneurship. Before joining the faculty at Wake Forest, Cohen was on faculty at Cornell from 2007 to 2015, where he founded and directed eLab, Cornell's entrepreneurship accelerator program hailed by *Forbes* magazine as a major driver of Cornell's ascent to a #4 national ranking in entrepreneurship. In 2012, Cohen was awarded Cornell's Robert N. Stern Memorial Award for Mentoring Excellence. His academic career began in 2005 when he accepted a faculty appointment at The University of Iowa's Tippie College of Business. While at The University of Iowa, Cohen earned accolades for teaching, advising, and mentoring excellence. Cohen earned his PhD in management from Case Western Reserve University. He studies how nascent entrepreneurs develop a passion for entrepreneurship and how, and under what conditions, they form an entrepreneurial identity. He also researches how entrepreneurs develop key capabilities, such as how to spot and develop valuable opportunities.

Before his academic career, Cohen had a successful 15-year entrepreneurial career that included founding, growing, and successfully exiting his startup in 2005.

Greg Pool, JD, MBA, is a lifelong entrepreneur. He started businesses during college at the University of South Carolina Honors College and while attending Wake Forest University for law school and business school. Greg has founded and cofounded several businesses that he has exited, as well as leading turn-around and relaunch efforts. Greg was the entrepreneur-in-residence at Wake Forest University before becoming director of Wake Forest's startup accelerator, Startup Lab, which he cofounded with Dan Cohen. Greg is now a member of the entrepreneurship faculty at Wake Forest, where he specializes in helping entrepreneurs create early value in their companies. In 2017, he was awarded the Russell D. and Elfriede Hobbs Faculty Award for Exceptional Support of Entrepreneurship.

Heidi Neck, PhD, is a Babson College professor and the Jeffry A. Timmons Professor of Entrepreneurial Studies. She is the academic director of the Babson Academy, a dedicated unit within Babson that inspires change in the way universities, specifically their faculty and students, teach and learn entrepreneurship. The Babson Academy builds on Neck's work starting the Babson Collaborative, a global institutional membership organization for colleges and universities seeking to increase their capability and capacity in entrepreneurship education, and leading Babson's Symposia for Entrepreneurship Educators (SEE), programs designed to further develop faculty from around the world in the art and craft of teaching entrepreneurship and building entrepreneurship programs. Neck has directly trained more than 3,000 faculty around the world in the art and craft of teaching entrepreneurship.

She has taught entrepreneurship at the undergraduate, MBA, and executive levels. Neck is a past president of the United States Association of Small Business and Entrepreneurship (USASBE), an academic organization dedicated to the advancement of entrepreneurship education. Her research interests include entrepreneurship education, the entrepreneurial mindset, and entrepreneurship inside organizations. An award-winning educator and author, her textbook *Entrepreneurship: The Practice and Mindset* (2017) was awarded Breakthrough Book of 2017 by SAGE and the 2018 Most Promising New Textbook award by the Textbook & Academic Authors Association.

Neck is the lead author of *Teaching Entrepreneurship: A Practice-Based Approach* (Elgar), a book written to help educators teach entrepreneurship in more experiential and engaging ways. Additionally, she has published 45+ book chapters, research monographs, and refereed articles.

Neck has been recognized for teaching excellence at Babson for undergraduate, graduate, and executive education. She has also been recognized by international organizations the Academy of Management and USASBE for excellence in pedagogy and course design. For pushing the frontiers of entrepreneurship education in higher education, The Schulze Foundation and the Entrepreneur and Innovation Exchange awarded her Entrepreneurship Educator of the Year in 2016.

1

INTRODUCTION

A rival coach had this to say about legendary Alabama football coach Bear Bryant: "He can take his team and beat your team, or he can take *your* team and beat *his* team."

Clearly, raw material did not matter to Coach Bryant. He could mold a good team out of whatever players he happened to be coaching, regardless of talent. Similarly, great poker players can win despite a poor hand. Less experienced coaches and poker players—those lacking in expertise—require a better team or a better hand in poker in order to succeed.

All of the above holds true for the best entrepreneurs. Because of their knowledge and experience, they see trends where others just see data; they see patterns when others see chaos; they connect dots when others just see dots. This ability to consistently recognize and seize opportunity develops over time and with practice. Though extensive industry experience and a strong professional network are crucial, most aspiring entrepreneurs, especially students, do not have the advantage of domain expertise, industry background, or a strong network. Like novice poker players, they have better odds of succeeding if they start with a strong hand. This workbook helps beginning entrepreneurs overcome some of these challenges by providing a proven method to generate entrepreneurial opportunities—ideas that can produce real value.

Generating new ideas and evaluating their value is at the very core of entrepreneurship.[1] The great news is that the ability to spot problems, develop new ideas, and evaluate their value as potential entrepreneurial opportunities is a skillset that can be developed, and we are going to help you do just that. In fact, this essential skillset should be developed even before other skills, such as producing a business plan or a feasibility study, are addressed.

When you don't necessarily have knowledge and experience, it can seem very difficult to know whether an idea has the potential to reach the market and develop into a viable venture. Aspiring entrepreneurs tend to focus on novelty and what's new to the market, while more experienced entrepreneurs focus on profit potential and market size.[2] Nascent entrepreneurs often think their ideas are strong simply because they don't have the requisite knowledge to prove otherwise. As a result, too much time and too many resources can be wasted on a "not so good" idea.

For example, you might have an idea for a great new app, but did you know that there are currently 2 million apps available? How will you stand out? Why is your app different? How will you get users? If you've never built a profitable app, how do you know what you don't know? This workbook is designed to help you achieve a much better rate of success by insisting you start out with strong, high-potential ideas. You will generate these ideas by using an empirically proven method to spot, evaluate, and select great ideas: the IDEATE method.

IDEATE is an acronym, with each letter denoting an important component in the framework designed to help you develop a skillset to identify valuable opportunities (see Table 1.1).

Table 1.1

Identify	• Identify a "migraine headache" problem worth solving. • Distinguish between high-quality, exemplar opportunities and low-quality, uninspired ideas. • Begin to develop a sense of what makes ideas valuable versus ideas that are not worth the time and effort to explore.
Discover	• Actively search for opportunities in problem-rich environments. • Leverage your passions and areas of extreme curiosity to spot problems. • Explore current trends that are getting a lot of attention.
Enhance	• Add innovation and novelty to enhance existing opportunities. • Develop a "value for all" mentality to ensure all stakeholders are invested in your opportunity. • Experiment with alternative business models to increase value.
Anticipate	• Use the four sources of change to anticipate new opportunities: social and demographic, technological, political, and regulatory. • Examine how these changes affect existing markets and create new markets. • Anticipate customer needs that are likely to emerge as a result of future changes.
Target	• Identify target customers and understand their unmet needs. • Explore and connect with early adopters to better understand why they are buying and what resonates most with them. • Personify your ideal or typical customer.
Evaluate	• Practice scoring, selecting, and defending high-quality ideas. • Circumvent confirmation bias and other cognitive biases to avoid falling in love with bad ideas. • Avoid the excessive optimism trap and use critical thinking to evaluate ideas.

IDEATE has been validated through quantitative and qualitative research.[3] Qualitatively, numerous ideas generated using this method have developed into validated concepts and, in many cases, into high-potential ventures created by student entrepreneurs. Quantitatively, the IDEATE method has been empirically tested against a very popular approach to teaching opportunity identification (one some consider to be the previous gold standard) in an experiment across six university-based entrepreneurship courses. That experiment showed that the IDEATE method generated significantly more innovative ideas than the control method.[4] Bottom line: IDEATE is a proven method that was found to be significantly more effective than other ideation methods. Furthermore, we use it daily and we know it works!

HOW TO USE THE IDEATE METHOD WORKBOOK

This workbook is a method. Each component of the IDEATE framework builds on the previous one. IDEATE is a system of interconnected parts that, together and sequentially, create a path forward. That's why we recommend working through each component of IDEATE in the order presented. If you do, you will have identified 100 valuable opportunities by the time you complete this workbook.

Chapter 2 (Identify) will help you recognize what makes an idea valuable (or have real potential). You will learn about exemplars—ideas that are valuable along with what makes them valuable—as well as ideas that have not proven to be as valuable. You will start to record problems and engage in exercises designed to help get to the root cause of problems because deeply understanding a problem is the essential first step toward identifying possible solutions. Once real, "migraine headache" problems are identified, the idea generation process can begin. At the conclusion of Chapters 2 through 6, you will be asked to create 10 new valuable ideas and, using our ranking system discussed in this chapter, rank them from 1 (most valuable) to 10 (least valuable).

Chapter 3 (Discover) expands your search zone for valuable opportunities. Entrepreneurs spot and solve problems for customers. What are some fruitful areas where you might discover such problems? Beginning with activities that you engage in and are passionate (or at least curious!) about, you will look for problems you have encountered while engaging in these activities. Next, you will reflect on your own life experiences as potential idea sources. Perhaps you have studied abroad. Did you notice any successful business ideas in other locations that are not available to your home market? Years ago, a student named Howard Schultz simply could not find the European espresso café experience he encountered while studying abroad in Italy when he returned home to the United States. This gap prompted Schultz to launch the business that is now Starbucks. By utilizing analysis exercises like this, you will generate more ideas in Chapter 3 on your way to recording 100 valuable entrepreneurial opportunities.

In the book's fourth chapter, Enhance, we suggest ways of taking a problem or opportunity and enhancing it in innovative ways to create more value. Often, with a bit more effort, we can take our ideas and find "hidden" value that can be used to dramatically improve them. In other words, there are techniques that can be practiced to turn smaller ideas into bigger and bolder ideas. Alternatively, sometimes your idea may already be valuable, but a simple tweak may be what is needed to help the idea reach its fullest potential. The material and exercises in Chapter 4 will guide you through this process.

Chapter 5 (Anticipate) celebrates change. Although some fear or avoid change, strong idea generators and entrepreneurs see change as an ongoing fountain of new opportunities. Changes, such as social and demographic changes, technological changes, political and regulatory changes, and changes in industry structure, all create a never-ending stream of entrepreneurial opportunity for those astute enough to anticipate them and the impact they will have on customers, markets, suppliers, and industries.[5] Chapter 5 offers several exercises that feature changes that are on the horizon, allowing you to begin developing the skill to anticipate new opportunities that might emerge for each possible change. And don't depend on us to simply tell you about all the changes that are on the horizon—you will also be asked to research and identify other sources of change and further anticipate emergent opportunities.

Chapter 6 (Target) helps you think critically about the most important question entrepreneurs must answer: To whom are we selling and why should they buy from us? Startups do not typically have a known brand name, a strong stream of recurring revenue, a sales force, or any of the other complementary assets that larger companies enjoy. Lacking these resources, startups need to reach their intended target with pinpoint precision, in contrast to the large, established companies that can use a more diffuse approach to reach multiple segments. This chapter focuses on identifying the target market—the customers who have the greatest need or interest in what you have to offer and who rely on reports of the user experience when making buying decisions. Further, a clearly defined target establishes yet another path to viable ideas. What other needs for products or services might this market have? What products or services related to the initial idea might this target market also covet? Simply having a prototypical customer in mind helps you think about the customer's needs in an empathetic manner. These are all elements of the Target component of the IDEATE method.

Equipped with a decent pool of ideas, it's now time to develop your capacity to separate the good from the not-so-good. Chapter 7 is all about how you Evaluate—the second "E" in the IDEATE framework. However, you've been evaluating all along: At the conclusion of each chapter, you will be asked to calculate a score based on the size of the problem, your enthusiasm for the solution, and a gut feeling. However, in Chapter 7 you will learn a two-step process to more critically evaluate your top 10 ideas in order to narrow down the pool to three valuable ideas.

By the time you get to Chapter 8, you will have 50 ideas that have been narrowed down to three higher potential ideas. Now, armed with the new skills and knowledge acquired from Chapters 2 through 7, you will be asked to produce an entirely new set of 50 ideas. As in Chapter 7, you'll be asked to evaluate your top 10 ideas and choose three.

As you enter Chapter 9, you will have a six high-potential ideas that are worthy of further consideration. These six ideas will be sent through a few additional "checks" to help you choose one idea to articulate through the creation of an Idea Board.

A FEW FINAL WORDS BEFORE YOU GET STARTED

You will be generating a lot of ideas—at least 100 ideas worthy of evaluation—by the time you complete this book. Be prolific. Be creative. Take risks. Accept the challenge. You will find places to record your ideas throughout the book. That's why we have called it a workbook!

You will not, however, be asked to generate all 100 ideas at once. Our method is done in increments of 10 ideas. After completing each chapter, take some time for self-reflection. How much time did you spend generating those 10 ideas? Where did your ideas come from? What do you think of the quality of this batch of ideas? What might be fertile ground for finding new ideas? Can you look at these ideas and improve them in any way? Try to make your next 10 ideas better than your first 10. Note that you will develop 50 ideas throughout the first seven chapters of this workbook, and you will add 50 more through your work in Chapter 8.

If you wind up with *one* valuable, high-potential idea in Chapter 9, you've done it! And remember: You have the most to gain from maximizing your effort when following this proven framework.

IDEATE is an empirically proven method, but like any systematic approach, it is input dependent—if you have poor-quality input, you are likely to have poor-quality output. Ask yourself: Are you putting in the necessary time? Are you actively searching fertile ground for valuable ideas? Are you following the rest of the framework to the best of your ability? Try to make each batch of 10 ideas improve in quality and potential. Strive to have so many high-quality ideas that winnowing them down through evaluation is the hardest part of the framework!

2

IDENTIFY

The IDEATE framework is about generating high-potential, valuable ideas, but what is a valuable idea? People are not simply buying products or services; they are buying solutions to problems. It is the solution that is valuable.

WOULD YOU RATHER SELL VITAMINS OR ASPIRIN?

Although a market exists for both vitamins and aspirin, consumers are more likely to buy aspirin when they have a splitting headache than purchase vitamins to take over the long term for health effects that are hard to notice. But understanding what makes for a genuine "headache" problem—a real migraine that needs immediate attention—is not necessarily intuitive to all aspiring entrepreneurs. Without proper training, you are more likely to come up with problems that are matters of slight inconvenience rather than real headaches that *need* to be solved with customers who are just waiting for you to offer them a solution. When you have customers, you have a business. When you have a cool idea with no customer, well, you just have a cool idea. Student entrepreneurs sometimes think that identifying a problem that has no known solution is a good sign, when it might simply be that the problem was not substantial enough in the first place to demand a solution.

FIND A MIGRAINE HEADACHE AND YOU MAY HAVE FOUND A NEW BUSINESS!

By the end of this chapter, you will be able to identify a true headache problem. You will learn to differentiate between problems that customers will likely pay to solve and those that they likely will not care about. This can be a real sticking point for nascent entrepreneurs. Research shows that aspiring entrepreneurs have a tendency look for novelty (i.e., no one is solving this problem!) while experienced entrepreneurs look for margin and profit potential.[1]

Rather than inventing a problem for your solution, a better approach is to identify a problem that customers are currently trying to solve and are spending money to solve, but that is still not solved to the customers' satisfaction. When you find a problem like this and can solve it, you will find customers.

Here's an example. NORI is a startup that recently completed Startup Lab—Wake Forest's startup accelerator program. The NORI team noticed that women living in small, crowded city apartments often had wrinkled garments, but they did not have room for ironing boards, nor did they even own an iron. Discovering a wrinkled blouse in the morning means no time for dry cleaning. The NORI team noticed that with no iron or dry-cleaning option, women were using hair straighteners to "iron" their blouses! Because hair straighteners have no temperature control, they often would get too hot and burn the garment. Not only did this ruin clothes, but it also posed a significant safety hazard!

Even more frustrating was the fact that the hair straighteners didn't even get the job done; they were too narrow and small to adequately remove wrinkles from a blouse. So, these women were spending money on an inferior solution to a real problem. Can you say "migraine headache with an existing customer base"? Absolutely! NORI was created as an enhanced version of a hair straightener-turned-iron, a product that is temperature-controlled and significantly wider and longer than a hair straightener in order to iron a blouse quickly, effectively, without an ironing board, and with no risk of fire! In this case, the problem existed and customers were themselves trying to solve it in the absence of a workable solution. It was a situation ripe for a viable business idea and NORI received immediate validation from target market customers because they had identified a headache problem and offered a better solution.

THE COFFEE CONUNDRUM: EASILY SOLVED = NOT VALUABLE

Another clue, or rule of thumb, is that most "headache" problems are not easily solved in five minutes. For example, it's not uncommon for student entrepreneurs, like yourself, to come up with small-scale campus-based ideas for products and services. One simple example we've seen in our courses is a coffee delivery service. On the surface, the problem seems to be big: Students want to sleep as late as possible and still get coffee prior to class. The student either gets the coffee and is late or goes to class desperately in need of caffeine. Though the problem is real, is a coffee delivery service a valuable solution? This is a classic example of a "can be solved in five minutes" problem. By waking up five minutes earlier, the student can get coffee and be on time to class. Ideas of this sort do not typically add much value. Simply put, in most cases, when something is easily solved, it is not valuable.

Work to identify problems that, like the hair straightener/iron, people are paying to solve but are still unhappy with the results. These problems remove one obstacle in the typical idea generation process—finding paying customers. If they are paying for an inferior solution, they are quite likely to pay (and pay more) for a better solution.

There are other challenges related to opportunities that have a low chance of succeeding (not zero chance—never zero! The market sometimes likes pet rocks and fidget spinners!):

- ideas with tiny, niche markets

- ideas with unclear value propositions

- ideas that struggle to identify who the customer is

- ideas that do not bring anything of real value or uniqueness to the world

- ideas that are really features of a larger, established product

- ideas that have low or no barriers to competition

We will discuss each of these challenges with the hope that by the end of this chapter, you will have developed a strong "sense of smell" as to what makes an idea valuable.

DON'T PITCH NICHE: SIZE MATTERS

Ideas geared toward small niche markets often struggle to gain traction for several reasons. First, a small market can be saturated very quickly, and once the market is saturated, it is hard to grow or make a profit. From an idea standpoint, it can be difficult to get investors excited about making such an investment. For example, the pharmaceutical industry struggles to create drugs for rare diseases because the number of prospective customers is so low that it can be a challenge to produce and distribute products profitably to such a small market.

What makes an idea a niche idea? Simply put, the problem identified impacts a relatively small number of people. For instance, there are currently 16 million college students studying in U.S. colleges. The total U.S. population is 327 million, so college students make up about 4% of our population. If an idea services some small subset of college students, you are dealing with a niche market.

Conversely, a large market exists when a substantial portion of a population has a need. For instance, cell phones are a large market and appeal to most citizens. In the financial industry, Vanguard sells low-cost mutual funds. This means there are many different types of investors attracted to their products, from college students just starting to invest, to middle managers hoping to build a retirement nest egg, to extremely wealthy individuals who want a good return and low fees. The obesity epidemic in the United States has led pharmaceutical companies to create multiple drugs for diabetes, blood pressure, and other health problems related to obesity. Unfortunately, that market is only growing worldwide.

Identifying a large market allows room for pivoting or a change of direction if your initial idea is flawed. All things being equal, your idea has a much greater chance of thriving in a large, rather than a small, market.

DO WE REALLY NEED A NEW SHOPPING CART?

Another challenge that plagues opportunity quality is a murky value proposition. One idea that we see students identify with great consistency is a modern grocery-shopping cart. Students complain that it is inefficient to grocery shop, and they often have to go back to the same aisle on multiple occasions to get different items on their list. Our students have even measured how much time they waste walking aimlessly through the store—about 15 minutes. The solution to this problem seems obvious, they think: Let's upfit an existing grocery cart with an iPad that can connect with your shopping list and map an efficient route through the store.

Not so fast. There are several challenges to this idea, and most can be traced to its value proposition. First, what is in it for the grocery store? They are in a notoriously low-margin, highly competitive industry. Why would they want to spend significant capital to add expensive technology to their grocery carts, especially when impulse buys are something they depend on? Does the grocery store even care to solve this problem? Think about how many impulse purchases could be made in 15 minutes of aimlessly wandering the store!

We know what you're thinking. Grocery store customers would probably love to have technologically modified carts. Perhaps so, but would they like this experience enough to pay a premium to cover the cost? This takes liking something to a different level. Perhaps tech-savvy customers would like the carts, but non–tech savvy customers might cling to the status quo. Ultimately, the value proposition (i.e., who gets value from a new product or service and why) of this particular idea is ambiguous.

It helps dramatically if you can clearly articulate your value proposition in order to describe the problem, who would benefit most from the solution, and why. If you find these questions hard to answer, it may be a sign that you need to go back to the problem and understand it at a deeper level.

GO FIND THE HUMANS WHO ARE WILLING TO (AND CAN) PAY

Another area that creates challenges to idea quality is customer identity—specifically, a lack of clarity about that identity. A customer is a human being who has a problem (a want or need) and can pay for a valuable solution. For example, a hospital is not a customer. However, someone within the hospital system is. You should be able to answer the question, "To whom am I selling and why should they buy from me?" If you don't know the answer, well, you'd better go find it because if you do not know who your customer is, then customer discovery will be quite difficult.

Case in point: A startup once reported that they tried to get feedback on their medical device from a group of surgeons. They spent an entire year trying to get a meeting with these busy surgeons. Finally, they were able to sit down with the surgeons, who quickly informed the entrepreneurs that although they liked the medical device a great deal, the purchasing decision was made by the insurance company. A year of effort was lost due to a lack of clarity around the customer.

BRING SOMETHING TO THE WORLD THAT CANNOT EASILY BE OBTAINED ELSEWHERE

Ideas that fail to bring any real substantive value to the world—or, put another way, that do not bring anything to the world that cannot easily be obtained elsewhere—typically fail to gain traction. This is one reason why restaurants and retail share a morbid combination of high failure rates and low profit potential. If you have a restaurant concept that is not unique in some meaningful way, customers are much more likely to continue to patronize an established restaurant where they have a previous relationship.

In addition to the difficulties of trying to get customers to engage, it is also extremely difficult to earn healthy profit margins with products or services that are not well-differentiated. If two products are largely similar, customers only have one variable to distinguish between the two, and that is price. If companies compete on the basis of price alone, it is a "race to the bottom," and both companies ultimately suffer. It is extremely important at the idea stage to create something of value. In order to do this, you have to bring something new to the world that cannot easily be obtained elsewhere from companies that are already established.

WOULDN'T IT BE GREAT IF...? NOT REALLY

In their quest to spot and solve problems, aspiring entrepreneurs often note problems that are actually part of, or a feature of, an existing product. For instance, a commonly reported problem is that content available on Netflix, Amazon, network television, and so on, is not rated by friends of the viewer but instead by a very broad population of viewers. As a result, the algorithm ratings are not very effective at suggesting content. The solution might be a feature added to one of these existing companies or networks.

Another common example is ideas that spring from questions like "wouldn't it be great if we could do X on Instagram (or Snapchat, Facebook, Amazon, etc.)." However, it's difficult, if not impossible, to add features to existing products offered by another company. Further, the feature alone does not offer enough value to sustain itself as a standalone product or service—and certainly not as its own business. Generally speaking, it is best to avoid ideas that are really product enhancements for other companies.

Whenever possible, it is prudent to generate ideas that can enjoy a competition-free period of time in order to get established. The first thought that probably comes to mind in this regard is to patent an idea. If that is possible, then of course that path might be best. However, other approaches have been used effectively by scrappy entrepreneurs. Take Soft Soap, the company that invented liquid soap. Concerned that competitors such as Johnson & Johnson or Procter & Gamble could easily imitate their product, they purchased all the pumps available on the market. This gave them about a six-month head start on those large, established companies—ample time to generate enough customer loyalty and profitable operations to be ready to compete against those big companies when they finally entered the market.

Startups are weak organisms and are not ready to take on large, established companies.[2] Ideas that present some barrier to competition (or entry) will give most startups significantly better odds of succeeding.

Now it's time to get to work. But don't forget: Look for ideas that solve migraine headache problems impacting large numbers of customers, and do so in a way that allows you to create barriers to entry. Be sure to have a clear vision of the customer. Be able to articulate and prove the value proposition to your target market. Finally, look for ideas that can stand alone and are not merely feature upgrades to an existing brand.

IDENTIFY PRACTICE

Below is an example of problem identification, followed by prompts in which you will be asked to figure out what an underlying problem may have been, how potential customers are "solving" the problem right now, and how to identify the root causes of the problem.

EXAMPLE: Dogs stink. Our lovable and adored best friends sometimes have an odor that not everyone enjoys. What is the real problem in this situation? Bad odor is not the problem. The dog's odor is more likely a *symptom* or a *consequence* of other root causes, and if we can identify the root cause, we will then identify the real problem that could lead us to a potentially valuable solution.

You may be thinking, "Dog odor is absolutely a real problem." But think about it this way: If we stopped only at the fact that dogs can smell bad, we might decide that a new dog shampoo is needed. However, go to your nearest pet store and you will find dozens of dog shampoo options, all affordably priced and with mostly good reviews. There is shampoo to make your dog smell like peaches or pears. There is shampoo for the hypoallergenic dog. There is conditioning shampoo, low-suds shampoo, no-water shampoo, and organic shampoo. You name it. It's there. But what you might perceive to be the problem—dog odor—still exists.

After identifying the problem, it helps to identify how people are currently solving the problem. In the case of dog odor, assuming it actually is a problem, are dog owners ignoring it? Spraying doggie perfume on their animals? Going to a dog salon or groomer? Are they just bathing their dogs constantly? This is where doing some quick and early research, such as reading relevant social media groups or Reddit forums, can help you understand how customers may be currently addressing the problem and how these solutions are and are not meeting their needs.

To get to the real migraine headache you need to ask yourself, "Why is dog odor such a problem?" Soon you will start to see different root causes emerge.

> **Possible root cause #1**: Dog owners aren't bathing their dogs because the dog doesn't enjoy the process.
>
> **Possible solution #1**: Increase the dog's enjoyment of the bath by introducing new bath toys.
>
> **Possible root cause #2**: Dog hair clogs the bath drain and becomes a bigger problem itself, so the owner procrastinates about bathing the dog.
>
> **Possible solution #2**: Create a special strainer or circulator that eliminates this issue.
>
> **Possible root cause #3**: Bathing a dog just takes too much time, and owners aren't willing to put in the effort or simply don't have the time.
>
> **Possible solution #3**: A mobile dog-washing service that goes to the dog owner's house.

If considered, all of these possible root causes, and many more, would likely generate a better outcome for the entrepreneur than dealing with the symptom alone. If you think you've identified the real problem, always ask yourself "why is this problem occurring?" This self-interrogation is helpful in finding root causes.

In the following exercise, consider the following *symptoms* or *consequences* and identify their root causes in order to identify the migraine headache problem(s) that would yield higher quality solutions. Uncover three possible root causes and three possible solutions for each symptom or consequence below, just as we did with the dog odor example above.

Symptom A: Not following the manufacturer's recommended maintenance schedule.

Possible Root Cause #1:

_____

_____

Possible Solution #1:

_____

_____

Possible Root Cause #2:

_____

_____

Possible Solution #2:

_____

_____

Possible Root Cause #3:

_____

_____

Possible Solution #3:

_____

_____

Symptom B: The amount of chemicals Americans apply to their lawns in order to keep them looking green and "perfect."

Possible Root Cause #1:

_____

_____

Possible Solution #1:

_____

_____

Possible Root Cause #2:

_____

_____

Possible Solution #2:

_____

_____

Possible Root Cause #3:

_____

_____

Possible Solution #3:

_____

_____

IDENTIFY 10 IDEAS

Now it's time to put your new Identify skills to work and generate 10 ideas! Next, identify three problems (not symptoms or consequences) that *you* see. Remember, look for those "migraine headache" problems and look for any underlying causes of the problems, possible solutions that can turn into ideas, and how potential customers are dealing with the problems now.

You will be asked to describe each of your ideas in enough specific detail that someone could read it and understand the problem and solution without any additional information. To facilitate this level of detail, you will see four additional boxes below the description box.

The MHP Box: Assess the level or degree of the "migraine headache problem" (MHP) you have identified, using a scale of 1 (a small problem or minor inconvenience) to 5 (a true migraine headache problem).

The Enthusiasm Box: You may see an idea and believe it to be valuable, yet you may have no real personal desire to pursue it. Alternatively, if the problem you have identified and solution you have in mind addresses something you care deeply about or are interested in, you would probably also possess considerable enthusiasm to get it to market. In this box, assess your level of enthusiasm for your idea from 1 (not at all into this idea) to 5 (I'm really fired up about this idea).

The Gut Box: Entrepreneurs can see value or patterns in potential products or services that others simply miss. Sometimes this value is hard to describe or articulate and is often based simply on a feeling or an intuitive sense. This exercise will help you develop your instincts for spotting high-quality ideas. In this box, give your "gut" ranking from 1 (my gut says this is not a really big and profitable idea) to 5 (this is the next huge thing that everyone will be talking about and want).

The Total Box: This box will contain the overall score for your idea based on the three previous boxes. Total = (MHP × Enthusiasm) + Gut. For example, if the idea scored 3 on MHP, 5 on Enthusiasm, and 2 on Gut, my total would be (3 × 5) + 2 = 17.

You should now be able to rank your ideas from most valuable to least valuable in the batch. Please complete this table at the end of all chapters except Evaluate, where you will learn a more robust, critical thinking method of evaluating your top-ranked ideas. You may reuse a problem if you have more than one idea related to a specific problem. The goal is to generate 10 ideas.

Problem identified:			Rank (1–10)
Idea description:			Score
MHP (1–5):	Enthusiasm (1–5):	Gut (1–5):	Total ([MHP × E] + G):

Problem identified:			Rank (1–10)
Idea description:			Score
MHP (1–5):	Enthusiasm (1–5):	Gut (1–5):	Total ([MHP × E] + G):

Problem identified:			Rank (1–10)
Idea description:			Score
MHP (1–5):	Enthusiasm (1–5):	Gut (1–5):	Total ([MHP × E] + G):

Problem identified:			Rank (1–10)
Idea description:			Score
MHP (1–5):	Enthusiasm (1–5):	Gut (1–5):	Total ([MHP × E] + G):

Problem identified:			Rank (1–10)
Idea description:			Score
MHP (1–5):	Enthusiasm (1–5):	Gut (1–5):	Total ([MHP × E] + G):

Problem identified:			Rank (1–10)
Idea description:			**Score**
MHP (1–5):	Enthusiasm (1–5):	Gut (1–5):	Total ([MHP × E] + G):

Problem identified:			Rank (1–10)
Idea description:			**Score**
MHP (1–5):	Enthusiasm (1–5):	Gut (1–5):	Total ([MHP × E] + G):

Problem identified:			Rank (1–10)
Idea description:			**Score**
MHP (1–5):	Enthusiasm (1–5):	Gut (1–5):	Total ([MHP × E] + G):

Problem identified:			Rank (1–10)
Idea description:			**Score**
MHP (1–5):	Enthusiasm (1–5):	Gut (1–5):	Total ([MHP × E] + G):

Problem identified:			Rank (1–10)
Idea description:			Score
MHP (1–5):	Enthusiasm (1–5):	Gut (1–5):	Total ([MHP × E] + G):

SELF-REFLECTION ON IDENTIFY

Entrepreneurs are intense learners, and reflection is critical to their ability to move forward, iterate, and apply new knowledge. To help you develop your own reflection skills, record your answers to the questions below.

- Which idea surprised you most? Why?

_____

_____

_____

_____

_____

_____

_____

_____

_____

_____

- What was the most challenging aspect of the Identify section of the IDEATE method? Give a specific example related to a specific challenge.

_____

_____

_____

_____

_____

_____

_____

_____

_____

- What is your favorite idea? Is your favorite idea different from your highest ranked idea? Why?

  _____

  _____

  _____

  _____

  _____

  _____

  _____

  _____

  _____

3

DISCOVER

You may not believe you have what it takes to be the next Mark Zuckerberg, Sara Blakely, Sheryl Sandberg, or Elon Musk. Like many others, you may view these entrepreneurs as mythical beings who have overcome incredible odds to achieve unfathomable success. However, keep in mind that for every Mark Zuckerberg, there are millions of people we do not read about who are solving big problems and generating a lot of wealth for themselves and others. The truth is that many successful entrepreneurs have solved big problems that are actually somewhat simple in nature. The key is to spot the problem and act on it.

Successful entrepreneurs **discover problems and solve them**—it is as simple as that.

Action is key in demystifying the method of entrepreneurship. Once you begin taking action, you start developing confidence and proving to yourself that entrepreneurship is both accessible and doable. It is simply a matter of *discovering* problems that people will pay to solve. You don't have to discover a Facebook-sized idea in order to succeed. But even Facebook started small—on a single campus, solving the simple problem of connecting people more easily via technology.

Much has been written about the "aha!" moment—when an idea simply comes to you, perhaps in the shower or after a good night's rest. Those moments of inspiration may happen, but the odds of them occurring improve dramatically when an entrepreneur enters discovery mode and actively searches for headache problems to solve. In other words, you don't simply stumble on a problem in the shower; you work to find one.

In our Startup Lab Accelerator and in our classrooms, we advise our students to keep a log of problems they encounter in daily life as a way to spot valuable *organic* ideas, ideas for which *you yourself* are the customer because *you* are solving your own problem. Students often discover that many people also have that same problem. Netflix is a great illustration. CEO Reed Hastings forgot to return a movie he'd rented from Blockbuster and ended up paying a hefty fine. He wondered why movie rentals could not be rented on a subscription model like a gym membership. The idea behind launching Netflix was really that simple!

VIEW YOUR PROBLEM IN THE NEXT LARGER CONTEXT

Although solving organic problems is one valuable way of generating ideas, it sometimes leads to myopic fixes for small matters of inconvenience, rather than worthy solutions to genuine problems. One's own life can be used to generate good ideas, but the larger context in which an idea will take shape must always be kept in mind. For example, you might be an avid runner and have successfully completed five marathons. Perhaps your passion for running led you to read a book called

Born to Run by Christopher McDougall, a writer with a great passion for distance running. In this best-selling book, McDougall writes about the Rarámuri, prodigious distance runners who live in the remote Copper Canyons area of Northwestern Mexico. The Rarámuri will sometimes run up to 400 miles in a weekend! McDougall learned that they ran in "minimalist" sandals. As an avid runner and aspiring entrepreneur, you might have the idea that minimalist running shoes are a new opportunity.

As *Born to Run* topped bestseller lists, American runners began to wonder about training in minimalist shoes. It worked for the Rarámuri—they produced some of the best ultra-distance runners in the world—so maybe it could work for average runners, too. This led entrepreneurs to invent minimalist running shoes like the Vibram Five Finger shoes, which found an eager market. A growing industry now exists that, had it not been for McDougall's writing about the Rarámuri, might never have come into existence. And if the book hadn't been written and read by others, entrepreneurs would have not discovered the opportunity.

PROBLEMS IN YOUR PERSONAL SPHERE MAY HAVE LARGER APPLICATION THROUGHOUT THE WORLD

McDougall's own passion for distance running led him to the Rarámuri, which led him to writing the book that led others to create new markets. His discovery, though personal in origin, led to an idea that had a larger application in the world. McDougall's book also influenced another successful startup called Health Warrior. The founders of Health Warrior were endurance athletes who read about the Rarámuri runners and how they would eat chia seeds—an amazingly potent source of nutrition. Given the small serving sizes needed, these seeds were perfect for endurance athletes searching for powerful nutrients that come in small packages. This led to the creation of Health Warrior's small nutrition bars made of chia and other healthy nutrients. In a short time, Health Warrior grew to tens of millions in sales before being acquired by Pepsi in 2018. These examples suggest that new ideas come from not only identifying problems but also discovering new problems by actively searching for them.

To identify areas in which you can discover new ideas, answer these questions:

- What activities are you passionate about?
- What places in the world have you visited?
- Do you have areas of expertise?
- What problems do you encounter in your day-to-day activities?
- What current trends have you noticed that might yield valuable opportunities?

Answering these questions will prepare you for the exercises presented later in the chapter that will help you get into discovery mode.

SPEND TIME LEARNING MORE ABOUT YOUR FAVORITE ACTIVITY

In McDougall's book *Born to Run*, those passionate about distance running were able to discover two multimillion-dollar ideas just by paying attention to the facts outlined in the book! What activities are you passionate about? What activities do you partake in with great frequency? If you get great joy from these activities, it should be fun to engage in these activities, read about these activities, and talk to other people who are similarly passionate. What are some challenges you have noted about participating in these activities? What problems have arisen, and have you developed any work-arounds or low-fidelity solutions? Have others? What could be added to your favorite activity that could make it even more enjoyable?

Further, does your activity exist in other parts of the country? In other parts of the world? Is there an opportunity for you to teach this activity to others who would benefit from it? Is there an opportunity to scale it or to leverage technology to help it grow or reach others?

A TRIP TO ITALY BROUGHT US STARBUCKS

Howard Schultz greatly appreciated the warmth and vitality of the espresso cafés he frequented while studying abroad in Italy. Upon returning home to the United States, he could not find cafés that offered the same sense of community. That led him to create the business model that became what we now know as Starbucks.

Recall your own travel experiences. Did you note any opportunities there that do not exist in your own community? "Borrowing and refining" an idea from another part of world has one potent advantage—market validation. This doesn't guarantee that an idea that works in Santiago, Chile will work equally well in San Diego, but at least you have some data to start with. The fact that the idea has been embraced in one part of the world is certainly a good sign that it could be adopted in other parts of the world.

What ideas or businesses have you noticed while traveling or studying abroad that do not exist here or in other parts of the world? Reimagine your trips (certainly a fun exercise) and give thought to ideas you came across elsewhere that might work here.

WE ARE ALL AN EXPERT AT SOMETHING

Leveraging your talents or previous experience can also lead to new entrepreneurial ideas.[1] Growing up, perhaps you mastered some unique skillset and, as a result, developed deep knowledge. A great example of this comes from a former student of ours, Aaron Walls. Aaron loved brewing beer so he became an expert at it. While participating in eLab (Cornell's startup accelerator program), Aaron solved a big problem he had encountered as a college student interested in brewing: He did not have the space in his small apartment to brew beer. Beer must be kept cold during the fermenting process, and often home brewers will remove shelving in a refrigerator in order to store the beer container. In a small apartment, with no space for a second refrigerator, Aaron faced a challenge. He shared his problem with two of his roommates and, collectively, they wondered if they could make a mini-refrigeration unit that would cool just the liquid, eliminating the need to utilize an entire home refrigerator that cools the air *around* the liquid. They solved the problem by inventing the Brew Jacket—a small refrigeration unit that sits on top of a keg, with a metal stem that is inserted into the beer and cools the liquid only. This allows the home brewer to store the keg anywhere, eliminating the need for a traditional refrigerator.

This clever invention allowed for easy storage of kegs during the brewing process and opened up home brewing to those living in apartments or small homes, or those who simply wanted to use their refrigerators for more traditional purposes! Aaron and his roommates have gone on to develop other successful products in the home beer brewing space by leveraging Aaron's deep expertise in home brewing beer. What expertise or innate talents have you developed that you could leverage to solve problems?

WHAT GIVES YOU A MIGRAINE HEADACHE EVERY DAY?

Another generative area for opportunity identification is spotting and solving your own problems, with or without deep knowledge and previous expertise. This is a great way to develop ideas because you're solving a problem you've encountered personally, a great motivator for developing a valuable solution. One risk of this approach, though, is that you need to be able to differentiate between minor inconveniences and "migraine headaches."

Dana Lampert, founder of Wiggio.com, discovered a problem in his own day-to-day life that sparked a company. Dana, a very active college student at Cornell, had difficulty keeping track of all of his activities, social events, intramural sports, academic assignments, and other things related to college life. In order to solve this personal problem, he developed a calendar based on an idea he called WIGGIO—an acronym for "working in groups." WIGGIO kept all of his activities in a single online calendar, allowing him to share documents to work on group projects simultaneously and virtually. He could set text message reminders ahead of his commitments. It worked so well that he developed a company for the product.

Now, many of WIGGIO's features were already available as one-off solutions. However, Wiggio.com put them all together into one easy-to-use tech platform that targeted college students. Along the way, people warned Dana that Google might enter the market, and eventually, it did, but not before Wiggio.com raised $3 million, scaled the company, and ultimately had a successful exit.

Dana was successful because he simply noted a migraine problem that he had encountered in his daily life, and he solved it really well. What challenges and problems have you encountered in your daily life that are really problematic and need to be solved?

OBSERVE NEW NEEDS CREATED BY CURRENT TRENDS

Another way to discover valuable ideas is to examine current trends in the market and look for unmet needs these trends have created. Current trends abound! Augmented reality, advances in 3D printing, blockchain, cryptocurrency, and many other things are trending right now. What opportunities have emerged from these trends? What unmet needs do customers have that resulted from these trends? Let your mind wander about these trends and think about what they will mean to customers, and the ideas will begin to flow.

DISCOVER PRACTICE

Below are two stories of companies founded after their owners discovered a problem, as well as a little bit of the journey that took them to where they are today.

F'real Frozen Milkshakes: Who Knew the World Needed More Milkshakes?

Jim Farrell was in corporate sales for Edie's Gourmet Ice Cream. His job was to sell ice cream to restaurants. When he visited a restaurant or ice cream shop, he would ask the restaurant manager or owner how they could increase the sale of ice cream. The managers consistently identified a problem: Customers love milkshakes, but the wait staff hated making milkshakes! They complained that milkshakes were labor intensive because making them involved lifting heavy ice cream containers from the freezer and seemingly continuous scooping. But the same could be said for scooping out ice cream for sundaes. What made milkshakes even more annoying to make was that they took far more time than making cones—requiring the addition of milk and other ingredients, such as candy, caramel, or fruit. They were also messy. Milk might spill, ice cream might splatter during mixing, and the blender itself had to be cleaned after each use. In an industry where customer patience is short, these were major inconveniences for the wait staff.

After hearing about these problems again and again from multiple restaurants and shops, Jim thought the pattern seemed to indicate a migraine headache problem. He was convinced that if he solved it, he would find commercial success. So he invented the world's first self-cleaning, completely autonomous, milkshake-making machine, called f'real. Jim was right about his hypothesis: Twenty years after founding f'real, Jim successfully exited the business when he sold f'real to Rich Products Corporation, a multinational headquartered in New York. A truly great entrepreneurial success story that traces its origins to simply discovering a customer problem and solving it—nothing more to it!

Pancake Pillow: An Innovative Solution to a Perplexing Problem

Entrepreneur Marty Carmichael noticed a problem: Pillows were often too thick or too thin for his liking. In trying to find the perfect pillow for himself, he discovered a related problem: Pillows are hard to return because of hygiene issues. Marty thought about the nature of the problem, including the difficulty of changing the thickness of a pillow based on the consumer's preference, and came up with an innovative solution that sprung from an unexpected quarter: his love of pancakes. He thought of how pancakes can be stacked, and using that mental prototype as a visual, he designed the Pancake Pillow. If you want a thicker pillow, leave all "pancake" cushions in. If you want it thinner, simply remove a few "pancakes" until desired thickness is achieved.

The difficulty in varying the thickness of a pillow was the root cause that Carmichael identified. After that, he simply solved the problem.

Table 3.1 lists three companies that discovered opportunities that may not seem overly complicated, but that solved problems many customers had. Research these companies and try to identify the problems they solved, how the founders realized that there was a problem in the first place, and why their solutions resonated so much with their customers.

Table 3.1 Company Research Table			
	COMPANY DESCRIPTION	PROBLEM SOLVED	TARGET CUSTOMERS
DOLLAR SHAVE CLUB			
	COMPANY DESCRIPTION	PROBLEM SOLVED	TARGET CUSTOMERS
Casper ONE PERFECT MATTRESS			
	COMPANY DESCRIPTION	PROBLEM SOLVED	TARGET CUSTOMERS
SharkBite			

DISCOVER 10 IDEAS

Using the different techniques in this chapter, identify ideas that can be added to your list of 10 at the end of this chapter. Let's get started.

Identify three **personal experiences** that would give you insight into areas of opportunity:

	EXPERIENCE DESCRIPTION	THE BIG PROBLEMS	POSSIBLE SOLUTIONS
Experience 1			
Experience 2	EXPERIENCE DESCRIPTION	THE BIG PROBLEMS	POSSIBLE SOLUTIONS
Experience 3	EXPERIENCE DESCRIPTION	THE BIG PROBLEMS	POSSIBLE SOLUTIONS

Identify **challenges and problems you have encountered in your daily life** that are really problematic and need to be solved.

	DESCRIPTION OF CHALLENGE	THE BIG PROBLEMS	POSSIBLE SOLUTIONS
Challenge Encountered			
Challenge Encountered	DESCRIPTION OF CHALLENGE	THE BIG PROBLEMS	POSSIBLE SOLUTIONS

	DESCRIPTION OF CHALLENGE	THE BIG PROBLEMS	POSSIBLE SOLUTIONS
Challenge Encountered			

Identify **expertise or innate talents you have developed** that you could leverage to solve problems, and list three problems that you could solve that match up with those talents.

	DESCRIPTION OF EXPERTISE/TALENT	THE BIG PROBLEMS	POSSIBLE SOLUTIONS
Unique Expertise			

	DESCRIPTION OF EXPERTISE/TALENT	THE BIG PROBLEMS	POSSIBLE SOLUTIONS
Unique Expertise			

	DESCRIPTION OF EXPERTISE/TALENT	THE BIG PROBLEMS	POSSIBLE SOLUTIONS
Unique Expertise			

Identify **ideas or businesses you have noticed while traveling or studying abroad** that do not exist here or in other parts of the world.

	DESCRIPTION OF OPPORTUNITY	THE BIG PROBLEMS	POSSIBLE SOLUTIONS
Opportunities Noticed Elsewhere 1			

	DESCRIPTION OF OPPORTUNITY	THE BIG PROBLEMS	POSSIBLE SOLUTIONS
Opportunities Noticed Elsewhere 2			

	DESCRIPTION OF OPPORTUNITY	THE BIG PROBLEMS	POSSIBLE SOLUTIONS
Opportunities Noticed Elsewhere 3			

Identify the **activities you are passionate about.** What activities do you partake in with great frequency? What are some challenges you have noted about participating in these activities? What could be added to your favorite activity that could make it even more enjoyable? Is there an opportunity to scale this activity or leverage technology to help it grow or reach others?

	DESCRIPTION OF ACTIVITIES	THE BIG PROBLEMS	POSSIBLE SOLUTIONS
Passionate Activities 1			

	DESCRIPTION OF ACTIVITIES	THE BIG PROBLEMS	POSSIBLE SOLUTIONS
Passionate Activities 2			

	DESCRIPTION OF ACTIVITIES	THE BIG PROBLEMS	POSSIBLE SOLUTIONS
Passionate Activities 3			

Identify **current trends** that seem to be getting traction in the marketplace. What opportunities might these trends yield to those actively searching? For instance, the hotel industry has been challenged by Airbnb and others that followed the trend of renting out personal assets (homes, cars, etc.). It probably would not make sense to create a competitor to Airbnb (they would be tough competition out of the gate!), but perhaps opportunity exists for an Airbnb concierge service or other ancillary services that have been created by the trend of renting out your own space.

	DESCRIPTION OF CURRENT TRENDS	THE BIG PROBLEMS	POSSIBLE SOLUTIONS
Current Trends 1			
Current Trends 2	DESCRIPTION OF CURRENT TRENDS	THE BIG PROBLEMS	POSSIBLE SOLUTIONS
Current Trends 3	DESCRIPTION OF CURRENT TRENDS	THE BIG PROBLEMS	POSSIBLE SOLUTIONS

Now it's time to generate 10 new ideas based on the work you've just completed. The boxes with possible solutions above may turn into some good ideas for your next batch. Remember to score the MHP, Enthusiasm, and Gut boxes on a 1 to 5 scale. (MHP x Enthusiasm) + Gut equals your total. Once you have a score, then rank your ideas from 1 to 10.

Problem identified:			**Rank (1–10)**
Idea description:			**Score**
MHP (1–5):	Enthusiasm (1–5):	Gut (1–5):	Total ([MHP × E] + G):

Problem identified:			Rank (1–10)
Idea description:			Score
MHP (1–5):	Enthusiasm (1–5):	Gut (1–5):	Total ([MHP × E] + G):

Problem identified:			Rank (1–10)
Idea description:			Score
MHP (1–5):	Enthusiasm (1–5):	Gut (1–5):	Total ([MHP × E] + G):

Problem identified:			Rank (1–10)
Idea description:			Score
MHP (1–5):	Enthusiasm (1–5):	Gut (1–5):	Total ([MHP × E] + G):

Problem identified:			Rank (1–10)
Idea description:			Score
MHP (1–5):	Enthusiasm (1–5):	Gut (1–5):	Total ([MHP × E] + G):

Problem identified:			Rank (1–10)
Idea description:			Score
MHP (1–5):	Enthusiasm (1–5):	Gut (1–5):	Total ([MHP × E] + G):

Problem identified:			Rank (1–10)
Idea description:			Score
MHP (1–5):	Enthusiasm (1–5):	Gut (1–5):	Total ([MHP × E] + G):

Problem identified:			Rank (1–10)
Idea description:			Score
MHP (1–5):	Enthusiasm (1–5):	Gut (1–5):	Total ([MHP × E] + G):

Problem identified:			Rank (1–10)
Idea description:			Score
MHP (1–5):	Enthusiasm (1–5):	Gut (1–5):	Total ([MHP × E] + G):

Problem identified:			Rank (1–10)
Idea description:			Score
MHP (1–5):	Enthusiasm (1–5):	Gut (1–5):	Total ([MHP × E] + G):

SELF-REFLECTION ON DISCOVER

- Which idea surprised you most? Why?

  _____

  _____

  _____

  _____

  _____

  _____

  _____

  _____

  _____

  _____

  _____

- What was the most challenging aspect of the Discover section of the IDEATE method? Give a specific example related to a specific challenge.

  _____

  _____

  _____

  _____

  _____

  _____

  _____

  _____

  _____

- What is your favorite idea? Is your favorite idea different from your highest ranked idea? Why?

  _____

  _____

  _____

  _____

  _____

  _____

  _____

  _____

  _____

  _____

4

ENHANCE

Entrepreneurs expand their active search for valuable ideas by focusing on either enhancing existing ideas or creating novel ideas by adding an innovative twist. Some of the ideas you generated in Identify and Discover could probably be better with a little enhancement—early ideas typically need to be enhanced to meet the needs of customers.

ENHANCE TO TURN A NICHE IDEA INTO A BIG-MARKET IDEA

When Logan Harvey, a junior at Wake Forest University, presented his idea for an app to find the closest available parking on a college campus—an idea frequently generated at collegiate entrepreneurship programs—he used the IDEATE framework to enhance the idea in order to create more value in the marketplace for a larger set of customers. What he learned through his enhancement exercises was that the college student market at Wake Forest University was too small and too niche.

Rising to the challenge, Logan applied his idea to a larger market and enhanced his app to help businesses near stadiums rent their lots to those searching for parking. In a sense, it was Airbnb for parking lots. These businesses had been renting out their lots for years under a traditional setup in which an onsite lot attendant leases out the spaces on a first come, first serve basis. Logan's startup, called FanPark, enhanced this scenario by introducing dynamic pricing to a static market. By advertising the spaces to potential customers in advance and showing a dwindling number of available spots (similar to how airlines work), FanPark is able to command premium prices for spaces and collect revenue in advance of an event. Further, customers—especially those traveling for the event—are willing to pay a premium for the peace of mind of having a reserved spot. FanPark gets a portion of the newly created value, while ensuring that all parties share in it—key to attaining entrepreneurial traction.

TWIST AND SHOUT: "I'VE GOT SOMETHING AWESOME FOR YOU NOW!"

Kristen McClellan, founder of the SnappyScreen Sunscreen Application System, added a twist to an existing idea in order to come up with something new to the market. Kristen noted her friends were getting spray-tanned to give the appearance of having a deep, dark tan without having to spend time in the sun. The technology of a spray-on tan attracted a small niche market of college-age, appearance-oriented women. Kristen wondered, as good entrepreneurs do, if this technology could be enhanced to solve a greater problem: reducing skin cancer rates of people who spend time in the sun to get their tans.

Kristen noted that her spray-tanned friends would stand in a machine while the "tan" was sprayed on their bodies through nozzles. A victim of frequent sunburns, Kristen figured that if you could spray on a tan, you could also spray on sunscreen as protection. She noted that most people applied sunscreen incorrectly—spreading it unevenly and missing some parts of their exposed skin entirely. Thus, even when people applied sunscreen, they were not safe from the sun.

Over time, Kristen developed a method of applying sunscreen so that the skin was perfectly coated with the appropriate amount. Users walk into a "standing pod" and are sprayed with sunscreen, just as spray-tanners are applied. Kristen tested her method using infrared technology that highlighted any areas of the skin that were not protected, tweaking the SnappyScreen System until all areas of the body were perfectly coated.

SnappyScreen is now the world's first hands-free sunscreen application system that gives users full-body sunscreen coverage in 10 seconds! How awesome is that?

REIMAGINING THE OLD AS SOMETHING NEW

Entrepreneurs are often in a better position to enhance ideas and find new solutions to old problems than more established companies that are tethered to expectations established over time through the development of their brand.

For example, the circus industry was once struggling mightily. Animals, long central to the circus theme, were poorly treated, and circus companies found themselves under tremendous scrutiny by animal rights groups. Ringling Bros. was accused of abusing and mistreating the animals they used, which distressed audiences and kept them way. Changing perceptions about how circuses use exotic animals also led to lower attendance numbers. This, combined with shortened audience attention spans that made focusing on three rings problematic for young circus attendees, meant that even Ringling, a strong, well-established brand, was in trouble. However, perhaps because of their brand strength and customer expectations tethered to the Ringling Bros.-style circus, it was difficult for them to reimagine the circus experience.

Then, along came Cirque du Soleil with a significant enhancement to the circus experience. They reimagined the circus experience in a way that eliminated the need for animals and "three rings" of activity, two parts of the circus that no longer added value for audiences. In addition, they enhanced the circus experience by introducing more acrobatics and adding a theatrical element that attracted a more sophisticated, higher-paying clientele. In a sense, they created an adult circus experience and, by adding the thematic element, attracted repeated attendance from customers wishing to see the latest theme. They established profitable operations and worldwide expansion by enhancing an existing attraction—reimagining the old into something new.

One way to think more deeply about enhancing ideas is to broaden the lens to examine how different constituents, such as customers, suppliers, or other stakeholders, are impacted by the idea. Sometimes entrepreneurs can hyper-focus on customers and forget to extract value for themselves, and this is not really a sustainable path forward. Other times, entrepreneurs may focus on their own gain without enough focus on partners or suppliers that are essential to value creation. By taking a holistic view that encompasses all parties, opportunities to enhance ideas expand significantly. We have a simple way of thinking about this important concept: If it is not good for all, it is good for none.

BUILD VALUE FOR ALL, NOT JUST THE CUSTOMER

Cirque du Soleil is also a good example of value building not only for the customer but for others as well. They built value for activists (not using animals), performers (less danger and more creative content), and cities or venues (less liability without animals). As we have continuously stated, entrepreneurial opportunities must generate value. Efforts to solve the customer's problem must be additive and valuable to *all* seeking to solve it. We view this as a three-legged stool:

- Leg One: Provide significant value to your customers by solving their problem effectively.

- Leg Two: Add value to anyone else who helps you solve the customer's problem. This could be a supplier, a distributor, a delivery service, technical support, or some other component of the overall supply chain.

- Leg Three: Make sure that enough value is created for you, the entrepreneur, to benefit. If that does not occur, the entity is not sustainable. If an entrepreneur creates value, that value should be claimed by the entrepreneur(s). If value-creation does not result in a successful outcome for the entrepreneur, at some point the venture will fail, the value creation for customers and anyone else who participates in value creation will end, and no one wins. If you can't survive (financially), then why choose to do this? A clear path to profitability is essential.

If value is not created for all parties, then the chance of success dwindles significantly.

WOBBLY THREE-LEGGED STOOLS ARE NOT GOOD FOR ENTREPRENEURS

Most people do not know the story of a failed startup that was founded by the same people who created Priceline. The idea behind the failed startup was that the Internet could create leverage, to use the language of the time, or "democratize" shopping for the individual buyer. Customers who wanted to place an order for peanut butter, for example, would see Jif or Peter Pan as possible brands that they might receive, but they would not be able to choose a specific brand themselves. The startup would then aggregate all the orders for peanut butter and subsequently negotiate a very low price due to the increased buying power established by putting thousands of small orders together.

But there was a flaw in this business model. Peanut butter brands had spent millions of dollars building their brand. Why would they cheapen that brand to participate in a fledgling startup and sell their products for less? As a result, the brands chose not to participate because although there was value for the customer, there was no value for the suppliers. Without value generated for the big brands, the customers didn't matter.

HAVE A SEAT ON A STURDY, THREE-LEGGED STOOL

Silvercar is an example of a *sturdy* three-legged stool. The seed for the idea germinated on a men's golf getaway trip to California. After arriving at the airport and waiting to get their rental car, the group was dismayed to see that their rental for the weekend would be a white minivan. Even though the men's coolness factor dropped considerably, a new opportunity was born. The founders researched the rental car industry and wound up creating a valuable enhancement.

First, they looked into why renting cars is so expensive. It turns out that the rental car companies charge a lot for insuring vehicles, even though customers' existing car insurance already provides coverage. So, they enhanced the Silvercar model by taking insurance out of the equation. They simply asked their customers to provide proof of insurance.

Second, they realized that technology—particularly reservation technology—is a big component in terms of ease of reservation, logistics, supply and demand matching, and customer service. One of the Silvercar team members knew how to build these technology platforms from scratch, so they were able to compete in this space.

Finally, rather than purchasing fleets of different makes and models, they decided to approach a single automobile manufacturer to participate. Audi was interested because they saw a demographic change in the way people were purchasing cars and the traction that the sharing economy was gaining. Intrigued by this new way of selling cars and reaching different customers, Audi recognized a clear value proposition and agreed to sell cars to Silvercar at a discount. Silvercar wound up gaining significant traction in the market before successfully exiting to Audi after four years.

Let's review the value for everyone in this example. Silvercar was dissatisfied with the typical rental car experience—especially when it came to not knowing what car you were going to get. They enhanced the experience by finding an auto company that would provide the same car (an Audi!) for every rental. By cutting unnecessary insurance out of the equation, Silvercar could keep pricing reasonable. The customers win (always key!) because they know what they are getting (an Audi, not a minivan!) and that they are getting it at a reasonable price. Silvercar wins because they were able to grow a successful business and enjoy a fruitful exit. Audi wins because they grow and sell more cars and reach a different customer demographic. Clearly, we have a sturdy three-legged stool, as all parties received value by participating. In fact, Audi extracted so much value that they ultimately purchased Silvercar!

OTHERS' ENHANCEMENTS CREATE OPPORTUNITIES FOR YOUR ENHANCEMENTS!

Enhancing an idea can take other forms as well—a response to a market need created by another innovation, for example. eBay's rapid seizure of the online auction market created a lot of transactions between buyers and sellers who had no easy way to pay each other. PayPal's founders saw that the innovation created by eBay's online auction could be enhanced by adding a valuable service. Thus they solved a big problem for many people by creating a simple, easy, quick, and trustworthy mechanism for them to pay one other.

Another example of enhancement is provided by the startup E6PR (short for Eco Six-Pack Rings), which took a commodity product—the plastic rings that encapsulate six-packs— and replaced them with biodegradable, edible material. This solved a big problem—more than 50% of beer is sold in cans, and plastics like this litter the ocean and endanger sea turtles and birds. People are willing to pay a small premium to cover the costs and feel good about buying sustainable products.

ENHANCE PRACTICE

Table 4.1 shows three companies that enhanced some existing option or service. Research them and discover how they conceived and developed these enhancements:

Table 4.1 Enhance Practice Table			
	WHAT EXISTING PRODUCT(S) WAS(WERE) ENHANCED?	WHAT WERE THE ENHANCEMENTS?	WHAT PROBLEM WAS SOLVED?
SEGWAY			
hulu			
amazon			

ENHANCE 10 IDEAS

Now it's time to generate 10 ideas using the enhancement methods discussed in this chapter. A good starting point may be enhancing some of your ideas from the Identify and Discovery chapters. Additionally, you may look at existing products and services and enhance them to generate new ideas. As you did in previous chapters, score MHP, Enthusiasm, and Gut on a 1–5 scale, then create your total using the IDEATE formula of (MHP x Enthusiasm) + Gut. After scoring all 10 ideas, rank them based on score.

Problem identified:			Rank (1–10)
Idea description:			Score
MHP (1–5):	Enthusiasm (1–5):	Gut (1–5):	Total ([MHP × E] + G):

Problem identified:			Rank (1–10)
Idea description:			Score
MHP (1–5):	Enthusiasm (1–5):	Gut (1–5):	Total ([MHP × E] + G):

Problem identified:			Rank (1–10)
Idea description:			Score
MHP (1–5):	Enthusiasm (1–5):	Gut (1–5):	Total ([MHP × E] + G):

Problem identified:			**Rank (1–10)**
Idea description:			**Score**
MHP (1–5):	Enthusiasm (1–5):	Gut (1–5):	Total ([MHP × E] + G):

Problem identified:			**Rank (1–10)**
Idea description:			**Score**
MHP (1–5):	Enthusiasm (1–5):	Gut (1–5):	Total ([MHP × E] + G):

Problem identified:			**Rank (1–10)**
Idea description:			**Score**
MHP (1–5):	Enthusiasm (1–5):	Gut (1–5):	Total ([MHP × E] + G):

Problem identified:			**Rank (1–10)**
Idea description:			**Score**
MHP (1–5):	Enthusiasm (1–5):	Gut (1–5):	Total ([MHP × E] + G):

Problem identified:			**Rank (1–10)**
Idea description:			**Score**
MHP (1–5):	Enthusiasm (1–5):	Gut (1–5):	Total ([MHP × E] + G):

Problem identified:			**Rank (1–10)**
Idea description:			**Score**
MHP (1–5):	Enthusiasm (1–5):	Gut (1–5):	Total ([MHP × E] + G):

Problem identified:			**Rank (1–10)**
Idea description:			**Score**
MHP (1–5):	Enthusiasm (1–5):	Gut (1–5):	Total ([MHP × E] + G):

SELF-REFLECTION ON ENHANCE

- Which idea surprised you most? Why?

_____

_____

_____

_____

_____

_____

_____

_____

_____

- What was the most challenging aspect of the Enhance section of the IDEATE method? Give a specific example related to a specific challenge.

_____

_____

_____

_____

_____

_____

_____

_____

- What is your favorite idea? Is your favorite idea different from your highest ranked idea? Why?

_____

_____

_____

_____

_____

_____

_____

_____

_____

_____

5

ANTICIPATE

It is said that successful entrepreneurs live five years in the future. If change leads to entrepreneurial opportunity, then entrepreneurs can study changes and anticipate what these changes will yield in terms of valuable ideas. In order to have the best chance of identifying valuable ideas, you anticipate how changes happening today will impact the future.[1] Though most people don't like change, entrepreneurs thrive on it because with change comes opportunity. As you work through the IDEATE method, continue seeking out areas where ideas are most abundant in order to maximize the probability of identifying, evaluating, and selecting those ideas with the highest potential. Rather than passively examining problems encountered in their daily lives and recording them in a problem log, entrepreneurs utilizing the IDEATE method actively search for more fertile entrepreneurial ground.

Valuable ideas stem from four types of change: social and demographic, technological, political and regulatory, and changes in industry structure.[2]

ANTICIPATE SOCIAL AND DEMOGRAPHIC CHANGES

Hispanic Americans have overtaken African Americans as the most populous minority group in the United States. That fact, combined with the fact that there are more than 50 million U.S. citizens who consider Spanish their first language, means that this is a large, attractive market. These citizens may have unique needs or wants that entrepreneurs can satisfy.

We also have an aging population in the United States, which is leading to some real migraine headaches for the elderly and those who provide care for them. Yet, despite the real needs of this segment, very little entrepreneurial activity has targeted this valuable and growing demographic population.

The Pew Research Center has identified seven demographic trends shaping the world.[3] Their study is worth reading in its entirety, but here are three trends that stand out:

1. By 2020, there will be more Millennials on the planet than Baby Boomers.

2. One in five people in the United States is living in a multigenerational household.

3. Only 50% of U.S. adults are married, compared to 72% in 1960. Living together while unmarried is on the rise.

These demographic trends inevitably lead to social changes. For example, Millennials don't value ownership (of homes, cars, TVs, and other durables) as do Baby Boomers. As a result, we see the global emergence and success of new markets such as ride sharing (Uber), bike sharing (Lime), and subscription services (Netflix).

ANTICIPATE TECHNOLOGICAL CHANGE (BUT DON'T GEEK OUT)

Technological changes can simply be advances or changes in products or services that allow us to do things we could not do before or enable us to do them more efficiently. They also often result in cultural and social change. Ask your parents what their lives were like before the iPhone. What would you do without Uber or Lyft?

Opportunities can be found by creating new technology but also by looking at the impact of technology on the lives of others. For example, you may buy an iPhone from Apple (the technology), but where did you buy the case for your iPhone? An entire industry has developed just for phone and tablet cases.

Consider a few more examples of technological change:

- Augmented reality allows people to experience things in a manner not previously possible. People suffering from anxiety related to fear of heights, for example, can use augmented reality software to expose themselves to heights while in the comfort of their own home. In this way, they become desensitized to what they fear because they are exposed to it regularly in a controlled environment.

- The improving technology of solar panels, including reduction in size, has made them a common sight on houses and businesses thanks to their lower cost. This, coupled with increasing concerns about protecting the environment and negative effects of climate change, makes solar energy an area filled with opportunities.

- Recent advances in 3D printing allow companies to produce items directly from a 3D printer. Even large items like houses and boats have been 3D-printed!

ANTICIPATE POLITICAL AND REGULATORY CHANGE: ASK WHAT YOUR GOVERNMENT CAN DO FOR YOU!

Governments constantly take actions that impact business, as well as create spaces for new opportunities to flourish. When the U.S. government decided that all children under the age of 8 were required to use a child safety seat while traveling in a car, an industry was born. When the U.S. government decided to break up AT&T due to violations of anti-monopoly laws, ample opportunities opened up in the communications industry. Likewise, the deregulation of air travel led to the launch of companies like Southwest Airlines and Jet Blue.

Entrepreneurs who pay close attention to governmental actions that result in political or regulatory changes are rewarded with high-quality entrepreneurial opportunities. In addition to anticipating changes and identifying the new opportunities that result, entrepreneurs also need to look long term, especially for potentially negative effects. For example, Uber is fighting battles in cities all around the world as governments are trying to protect the taxi drivers whose livelihoods have been threatened by the rise of ride-sharing apps like Uber. In fact, Uber has been forced out of Barcelona entirely because the city government enacted a law stating that drivers cannot ride around looking for customers.[4] As a result, once an Uber driver completed a drive, they were forced to park at a centrally located garage, which destroyed the main benefit Uber offered its users: opening an app, hitting a button, and finding the closest ride. These "negative" changes could facilitate the birth of new ideas. For example, a new law could be created solely to protect the interest of car sharing services. Would Uber and Lyft pay for a law firm that specializes in this area? We think yes.

ANTICIPATE INDUSTRY CHANGES: DON'T FEED THE DINOSAURS!

The S&P 500 is an index of the 500 largest U.S.-based publicly traded companies. Historically the S&P 500 represented the oldest and most admired companies in the world. At the turn of the century, the average age of a company on the S&P was 60. Today the average age of an S&P 500 company is 20.[5] Amazon and Facebook are in the top 5 on the list, founded in 1994 and 2004, respectively. By Wall Street standards, these are very young companies. As a result, the cycle, or period of time, that an industry exists has diminished significantly over the past 20 years.

When an industry forms, many competitors pursue the newly created opportunities. Over time, the best firms rise to the top, and as they rise, they travel (and, hopefully, survive) a learning curve; that is, they make mistakes, they correct mistakes, and they develop a strong value proposition for customers. This makes well-established firms very difficult to compete with, as they have built loyal relationships with customers. Any new entrant to an established industry will have to take customers away from companies that have distinct advantages—a very difficult proposition for startups to overcome.

At the same time, large, established firms, particularly public firms that have shareholders, are typically quite averse to change. For them, change equals risk, and shareholders do not typically have much patience for things that threaten shareholder value. As long as things remain status quo in an industry, the established firms have many advantages. They have a brand name; they've suffered through the learning curve; they typically produce reliable products or services; they reinvest a portion of every sale in marketing programs designed to create future sales; and they have cash, profit, and other complementary assets that startups do not.

These established firms are heavily invested in the past and want to extract as much value as possible from their assets. This fact, combined with their risk-averse nature, makes them cling to antiquated approaches and shy away from exploring new approaches and technologies with which they are not familiar. For example, Blockbuster Video so heavily dominated video rentals that, when Netflix was 5 years old, Blockbuster earned more revenue from late fees than Netflix did in total sales! Blockbuster, though, was a retail play—their competitive advantage was that their stores were within a 10-minute drive of 80% of American homes. They were ubiquitous. Their dependence on a brick-and-mortar retail strategy meant that they did not focus on future shopping habits, such as renting movies via the Internet or simply streaming movies from home. In fact, their greatest strength contributed to their ultimate downfall when customers stopped going to retail stores to rent movies. There is only one Blockbuster still open in the world today and it's in Bend, Oregon. Only 15 years ago, Blockbuster had 9,000 stores.[6]

When an industry changes like this, the playing field is leveled, offering new entrants an opportunity to establish themselves. In effect, changes in industry structure give the upper hand to nimble startups that can rapidly evolve to meet customer needs. For instance, student entrepreneur Jake Reisch, who founded Eversound, cleverly adapted an existing technology known as the silent disco (visualize people dancing at a club with headphones and no external sound) to a much bigger market. Reisch applied this adapted technology to assisted living facilities, allowing patrons to better hear the movie being played each evening. By anticipating the needs of this growing market—Baby Boomers who are in, or will soon be in, nursing homes— Reisch was able to solve a real "migraine" problem: not being able to hear movies and not wanting to constantly ask others what was missed. He recently raised $3 million in venture capital to scale this idea nationwide.

ANTICIPATE PRACTICE

As we've seen, there are four broad types of change that present opportunities for entrepreneurs: (1) social or demographic change, (2) technological change, (3) political or regulatory change, and (4) market or industry change. In this exercise, you will practice identifying opportunities based on the four different types of change. First, for each of the four change categories, we have given you four examples of specific changes. Your job is to identify the headache problems associated with each change example and identify solutions to the headache problems. You may need to do a bit of research on each example to better understand the specific changes, so you can more easily uncover the associated problems. Then, we make it a bit more difficult. Armed with research and practice, next you need to find your own examples within each change category. As before, with each example you need to cite the headache problems and identify possible solutions. This is tough practice, so give yourself enough time. If you do the work, the quality of your output will be apparent!

Social or Demographic Change

Below are four examples of social or demographic changes. Research each example to uncover the headache problems. For each problem, identify a possible solution.

Social or Demographic Change	Headache Problems	Possible Solutions
1. The U.S. population is aging.	1. 2. 3.	1. 2. 3.
2. The U.S. population is becoming more pluralistic.	1. 2. 3.	1. 2. 3.
3. The U.S. population continues to suffer from negative health effects due to processed foods.	1. 2. 3.	1. 2. 3.
4. Millennials are living at home longer and delaying marriage.	1. 2. 3.	1. 2. 3.

Identify four more specific examples of social or demographic change, and for each example, identify the headache problems and corresponding possible solutions.

Social or Demographic Change	Headache Problems	Possible Solutions
1.	1. 2. 3.	1. 2. 3.
2.	1. 2. 3.	1. 2. 3.
3.	1. 2. 3.	1. 2. 3.
4.	1. 2. 3.	1. 2. 3.

Technological Change

Below are four examples of technological change. Research each example to uncover the headache problems. For each problem, identify possible solutions.

Technological Change	Headache Problems	Possible Solutions
1. Mobile devices capable of streaming digital video and audio inexpensively	1. 2. 3.	1. 2. 3.
2. Cheap, fast 3D printers able to print market-ready products on demand	1. 2. 3.	1. 2. 3.
3. Realistic and immersive augmented/virtual reality in people's pockets/homes	1. 2. 3.	1. 2. 3.
4. The need to store large amounts of demand-based electricity produced using renewable/green energy sources	1. 2. 3.	1. 2. 3.

Identify four more specific examples of technological change, and for each example, identify the headache problems and corresponding possible solutions.

Technological Change	Headache Problems	Possible Solutions
1.	1. 2. 3.	1. 2. 3.
2.	1. 2. 3.	1. 2. 3.
3.	1. 2. 3.	1. 2. 3.
4.	1. 2. 3.	1. 2. 3.

Political or Regulatory Change

Below are four examples of political or regulatory changes. Research each example to uncover the headache problems. For each problem, identify a possible solution.

Political or Regulatory Change	Headache Problems	Possible Solutions
1. California requiring some or all new construction to include solar panels	1. 2. 3.	1. 2. 3.
2. Restrictions on disposable plastic shopping bags	1. 2. 3.	1. 2. 3.
3. Political spending on the rise in elections	1. 2. 3.	1. 2. 3.
4. College athletics unionizing/ governmental involvement in student-athlete status	1. 2. 3.	1. 2. 3.

Identify four more specific examples of political or regulatory change, and for each example, identify the headache problems and corresponding possible solutions.

Political or Regulatory Change	Headache Problems	Possible Solutions
1.	1. 2. 3.	1. 2. 3.
2.	1. 2. 3.	1. 2. 3.
3.	1. 2. 3.	1. 2. 3.
4.	1. 2. 3.	1. 2. 3.

Market or Industry Change

Below are four examples of market or industry changes. Research each example to uncover the headache problems. For each problem, identify a possible solution.

Market or Industry Change	Headache Problems	Possible Solutions
1. Hotels having to compete with Airbnb-types who don't have to own a building but are still in the room-renting business	1. 2. 3.	1. 2. 3.
2. The "death" of Toys-R-Us and other toy-focused retailers	1. 2. 3.	1. 2. 3.
3. Consumers "cutting the cord" from cable TV for services such as Hulu and Amazon Prime	1. 2. 3.	1. 2. 3.
4. The replacement of the American workforce by computers/robots	1. 2. 3.	1. 2. 3.

Identify four more specific examples of market or industry change, and for each example, identify the headache problems and corresponding possible solutions.

Market or Industry Change	Headache Problems	Possible Solutions
1.	1. 2. 3.	1. 2. 3.
2.	1. 2. 3.	1. 2. 3.
3.	1. 2. 3.	1. 2. 3.
4.	1. 2. 3.	1. 2. 3.

ANTICIPATE 10 IDEAS

Now it's time to record and score your ideas. Your next batch of 10 ideas can come from the possible solutions you generated in the practice section, or you may start fresh. Whatever path you take, it's important that each new idea results from an anticipated change. As you describe your ideas below, really think about the problems and solutions you developed in the practice section above. It's time to start focusing on the *combination* of the problem and solution. A solution without a problem usually lacks customers. A problem without a solution is just a problem! So, a problem with a solution can be a powerful opportunity *if* people are willing to pay for the solution. Also, as you did in previous chapters, score MHP, Enthusiasm, and Gut on a 1–5 scale, then create your total using the IDEATE formula of (MHP x Enthusiasm) + Gut. After scoring all 10 ideas, rank your ideas based on score.

Problem identified:			Rank (1–10)
Idea description:			Score
MHP (1–5):	Enthusiasm (1–5):	Gut (1–5):	Total ([MHP × E] + G):

Problem identified:			Rank (1–10)
Idea description:			Score
MHP (1–5):	Enthusiasm (1–5):	Gut (1–5):	Total ([MHP × E] + G):

Problem identified:			Rank (1–10)
Idea description:			Score
MHP (1–5):	Enthusiasm (1–5):	Gut (1–5):	Total ([MHP × E] + G):

Problem identified:			Rank (1–10)
Idea description:			Score
MHP (1–5):	Enthusiasm (1–5):	Gut (1–5):	Total ([MHP × E] + G):

Problem identified:			Rank (1–10)
Idea description:			Score
MHP (1–5):	Enthusiasm (1–5):	Gut (1–5):	Total ([MHP × E] + G):

Problem identified:			Rank (1–10)
Idea description:			Score
MHP (1–5):	Enthusiasm (1–5):	Gut (1–5):	Total ([MHP × E] + G):

Problem identified:			Rank (1–10)
Idea description:			Score
MHP (1–5):	Enthusiasm (1–5):	Gut (1–5):	Total ([MHP × E] + G):

Problem identified:			**Rank (1–10)**
Idea description:			**Score**
MHP (1–5):	Enthusiasm (1–5):	Gut (1–5):	Total ([MHP × E] + G):

Problem identified:			**Rank (1–10)**
Idea description:			**Score**
MHP (1–5):	Enthusiasm (1–5):	Gut (1–5):	Total ([MHP × E] + G):

Problem identified:			**Rank (1–10)**
Idea description:			**Score**
MHP (1–5):	Enthusiasm (1–5):	Gut (1–5):	Total ([MHP × E] + G):

SELF-REFLECTION ON ANTICIPATE

- Which idea emerged that most surprised you and why?

_____

_____

_____

_____

_____

_____

_____

_____

_____

- What was the most challenging part about the Anticipate part of the IDEATE method? Give a specific example related to a specific challenge.

_____

_____

_____

_____

_____

_____

_____

_____

_____

_____

_____

- What is your favorite idea? Is your favorite idea different from your highest ranked idea? Why?

_____

_____

_____

_____

_____

_____

_____

_____

_____

_____

6

TARGET

Any ideas you've generated so far in this workbook are automatically worthless if customers are not willing to pay for a solution. Those who *are* willing to pay for your solution—who have a want or need and who consult one another in some way when making a decision—can be considered a target market.

NOT EVERYONE CAN (OR WANTS TO) BUY A TESLA

Elon Musk had an idea to build affordable, fun-to-drive electric vehicles for the masses. But at the idea stage, Musk realized that he did not have the economies of scale necessary to build a cost-effective electric vehicle. So instead, he targeted a smaller, more affluent market and smoke tested. Smoke testing is a way to gauge customer interest before building the actual product. You see this a lot online when entrepreneurs create a website for a product that looks launched but is not. The test enables you to estimate customer interest and more clearly define the target market. Musk smoke tested the Model S Tesla by posting a drawing of the car. With his drawing, he was able to presell millions of dollars' worth of cars that had not yet been built. Without having this clear target in mind, Musk would have solved a different problem for the wrong customer!

Later, based on what he learned from his smoke testing experiment, Musk developed the Model 3 for the middle- to upper-income consumer who wanted a Tesla but could not afford the Model S. In order to get market validation and capital to produce the new model, Musk targeted his new segment of buyers and asked them to pre-order the vehicle by placing a $1,000 deposit on the car. By securing millions of dollars in pre-orders through successful targeting, Musk validated his idea and moved into the production phase with more confidence and less risk.

With a clear target in mind, the entrepreneur can better determine customers' needs and identify their most pressing problems (i.e., the problems for which they will pay for a solution). For each idea you generate, make sure you clearly describe the target market. Remember, you have to ask the questions: To whom am I selling? Why should they buy from us?

START WITH A TARGET MARKET AND *LEARN LEARN LEARN* ABOUT THEM

In addition to the clarity that comes from having a well-delineated target market in mind as you create solutions to problems, the targeting process itself can be a catalyst for creating valuable ideas. Because the targeting process is about identifying a customer segment, studying those in the segment, noting headache problems they have, and creating solutions to resolve the headaches, the more disciplined you are about defining and understanding the group's makeup, the better able you are to gain insight into their wants and needs.

For instance, in the early days of Netflix, the company offered only DVDs, even though VHS was the dominant home-viewing medium of that era. But Netflix knew, based on its targeting research, that their customers would be early adopters of DVD players. As a result, it approached major manufacturers of DVD players and forged an agreement to have a Netflix coupon inserted in the box of every new player produced. Through effective and innovative targeting, Netflix was able to add value to the new purchase of a different product by providing a cool new service to their customer base. Further, by having a clear understanding of the makeup of their target market, they were able to reach them in a cost-effective way, and that is key for any resource-starved startup.

On a smaller scale, Driftwoods, a wonderful seafood restaurant in Aruba, realized that many of their customers were in Aruba to go diving and deep-sea fishing. The owner of the restaurant invested in a sport-fishing boat and took clients out deep-sea fishing. After catching the "catch of the day," the restaurant would keep the fish in exchange for a free dinner for customers who chartered the boat. Driftwoods understood that their customers wanted a unique experience rather than simply a dinner or even a deep-sea fishing outing. By offering both in an unusual and fun experience, the company was able to launch a related business that produced an additional stream of revenue while cleverly reducing one of their major costs—obtaining fresh fish for the restaurant.

Entrepreneurs who are able to acquire intimate knowledge of the unique needs of a target market are at an advantage in terms of discovering additional needs this market may have. Remember SnappyScreen from Chapter 4? After the success of their sunscreen application pods, SnappyScreen developed a line of sunscreen to sell to customers who may not be spending the day near the SnappyScreen Sunscreen Application machine. By knowing their needs and problems (not getting sunburned and not being able to easily transport sunscreen through airport security), SnappyScreen was able to develop a related product and help their target market customers simultaneously.

Another example of intelligent targeting can be found in the story of Can-Am, a company that builds fun vehicles. Their first vehicle, the Can-Am Spyder, was a trike (a motorcycle with three wheels that is fun to drive but significantly safer than a traditional motorcycle). Their target market (35- to 39-year-old married men with children who make more than $100,000 in annual income) wanted a fun weekend vehicle they could take for a Sunday afternoon ride and be home safely for dinner. Once Can-Am scaled this product, they began developing other lines of recreational vehicles that the target market would enjoy.

WATCH AND TALK TO PEOPLE IN A TARGET AREA TO LEARN ABOUT THEM. NO TEXTING. NO E-MAIL. NO FACEBOOK.

In order to learn about customer segments, you need to talk to individuals in those segments. Even better, watch them *and* talk to them. This is the only way to really understand and identify their headaches. For example, imagine you are in a motorcycle shop that buys and sells used motorcycles. On a particular Saturday, you notice men in their later 30s and early 40s coming in to sell their bikes rather than buy. You overhear one customer telling the store owner that his wife thinks motorcycles are too unsafe, given that they just moved to a busy city. You also overhear that he has three young kids. You can tell the customer is not happy to sell his bike. You may even develop the courage to ask him a few questions. What if you asked, "What is it that you liked most about riding your motorcycle?" He may answer that he just loved being so close to the road, the speed, wind in his face, or touring around on a sunny Sunday afternoon. Aha! How can you provide something to this target that gives them the same feeling with greater safety? Maybe this is how the Can-Am idea was born!

Entrepreneurs, whether in a for-profit or nonprofit structure, need customers to exist. By becoming intimate with customers and really knowing their wants and needs, entrepreneurs have a much greater chance of effectively solving their problems. Have you ever gotten a gift from a loved one that really misses the mark? Most people say yes to that question! If someone close to you can really miss badly on a gift, how can an entrepreneur pretend to have insight into what a market of strangers might want or need? The answer is that they cannot. In order to meet the needs of customers, entrepreneurs must become deeply familiar with the needs of their customers. Although customer discovery typically comes after the idea generation stage, when determining whether an idea is feasible, it is possible to learn a great deal about customer needs by reading reviews, reading bloggers or influencers who are well-regarded by target customers, and by visiting relevant social media groups in an effort to increase familiarity with prospective customers. If you do get an opportunity to talk to target market customers, then by all means make the most of it.

So what should you ask target customers if you are trying to find new headache problems? Four simple questions should get the job done:

Tell me *why* you are using _____?
Tell me *how* you are using _____?
What do you love most about using _____?
What do you like least about using _____?

TARGET PRACTICE

Below are three examples of products whose buyer (both the individual paying as well as the individual who makes or influences the buying decision) may not be immediately apparent. Think about who makes the purchasing decisions for these types of products. Recall the example from Chapter 2, when the surgeons had to tell the entrepreneurs that the hospital was not the customer—the insurance company was. Be careful not to confuse users with customers. In the IDEATE method, customers are people who pay money to solve problems. If you use Instagram, for example, you are a *user* of their product, not a customer. The customer is the advertiser.

As discussed, a target market is a group of customers who have a want or need and who influence one another in buying decisions. Try to describe this group using key demographic descriptors such as age range, income, gender, and any other characteristics that are relevant. Be careful to note that users are different from buyers. For example, if we want to purchase software in a university setting, we usually have to convince an administrator that we need the software. We are the users of the software but they are the buyers. So, in addition to being users, we also are influencers. We tell the economic buyers our preferences in hopes that they will buy the software we want. Entrepreneurs need to be ruthlessly efficient because of resource constraints. By focusing on the target customer and differentiating between users, influencers, and paying customers, entrepreneurs can proceed most efficiently. There is some trial and error here, for sure, and it can be puzzling at times trying to figure out who the decision maker is, but focusing on it from the start is key.

1. A new/improved stethoscope for a doctor or nurse

Likely User(s)	Likely Purchaser(s)	Influencer(s)

2. A new edutainment STEM toy targeting 6-, 7-, and 8-year-olds.

Likely User(s)	Likely Purchaser(s)	Influencer(s)

3. A Segway "Mini" (a hoverboard hybrid)

Likely User(s)	Likely Purchaser(s)	Influencer(s)

Now, flipping the script, the table below lists three potential target markets. In the space provided, suggest their headache problems and products or services that would specifically target those potential customers.

Possible Targets	Likely Headache Problems	Possible Solutions
Undergraduate college students living in a dorm		
Cruise passengers over the age of 70		
First-time parents who don't live close to other family members		

TARGET 10 IDEAS

For the batch of 10 ideas that follow, consider the ideas you generated in earlier chapters, paying particular attention to the target market those ideas would serve, and use them as catalysts to develop more ideas for the same target market. As you did in previous chapters, score MHP, Enthusiasm, and Gut on a 1–5 scale, then create your total using the IDEATE formula of (MHP x Enthusiasm) + Gut. After scoring all 10 ideas, rank your ideas based on score.

Problem identified:			Rank (1–10)
Idea description:			Score
MHP (1–5):	Enthusiasm (1–5):	Gut (1–5):	Total ([MHP × E] + G):

Problem identified:	Rank (1–10)
Idea description:	Score

MHP (1–5):	Enthusiasm (1–5):	Gut (1–5):	Total ([MHP × E] + G):

Problem identified:	Rank (1–10)
Idea description:	Score

MHP (1–5):	Enthusiasm (1–5):	Gut (1–5):	Total ([MHP × E] + G):

Problem identified:	Rank (1–10)
Idea description:	Score

MHP (1–5):	Enthusiasm (1–5):	Gut (1–5):	Total ([MHP × E] + G):

Problem identified:	Rank (1–10)
Idea description:	Score

MHP (1–5):	Enthusiasm (1–5):	Gut (1–5):	Total ([MHP × E] + G):

Problem identified:			Rank (1–10)
Idea description:			**Score**
MHP (1–5):	Enthusiasm (1–5):	Gut (1–5):	Total ([MHP × E] + G):

Problem identified:			Rank (1–10)
Idea description:			**Score**
MHP (1–5):	Enthusiasm (1–5):	Gut (1–5):	Total ([MHP × E] + G):

Problem identified:			Rank (1–10)
Idea description:			**Score**
MHP (1–5):	Enthusiasm (1–5):	Gut (1–5):	Total ([MHP × E] + G):

Problem identified:			Rank (1–10)
Idea description:			**Score**
MHP (1–5):	Enthusiasm (1–5):	Gut (1–5):	Total ([MHP × E] + G):

Problem identified:			Rank (1–10)
Idea description:			Score
MHP (1–5):	Enthusiasm (1–5):	Gut (1–5):	Total ([MHP × E] + G):

SELF-REFLECTION ON TARGET

- Which idea surprised you most? Why?

_____

_____

_____

_____

_____

_____

_____

_____

_____

_____

- What was the most challenging aspect of the Target section of the IDEATE method? Give a specific example related to a specific challenge.

_____

_____

_____

_____

_____

_____

_____

_____

_____

_____

- What is your favorite idea? Is your favorite idea different from your highest ranked idea? Why?

_____

_____

_____

_____

_____

_____

_____

_____

_____

7

EVALUATE

Up to this stage in the IDEATE method, you've learned what makes ideas valuable and you've practiced *identifying* headaches, *discovering* new opportunities, *enhancing* existing ideas, *anticipating* changes that lead to a new market, and *targeting* customer groups to better understand their needs. You have ranked each batch of ideas and have ranking scores for 50 ideas at this point. It is now time to more critically evaluate your ideas through a four-step process we introduce in this chapter. First, we'll cover some of the most important considerations that separate high-value from low-value ideas.

ARE YOU RESOLVING A MIGRAINE HEADACHE WITH A "PULL" SOLUTION?

We learned about problem identification earlier in the workbook. It makes sense that the size of the problem you're attempting to solve will have a strong role in dictating the success of your venture. If there isn't a willingness by customers to buy your product or service—because they feel they need it even more than they want it—then your potential sales volume will decrease alongside an increase in the cost to market/advertise.

A huge problem will make the customers "pull" your solution to them. In other words, just by virtue of offering it to the market you'll have built-in momentum and sales. A smaller problem will force you to "push" the solution onto would-be customers, attempting to convince them that they really do need to solve such a small (perceived) problem by using your solution. Pushing a customer is a lot more work than pulling a customer! The degree of pull is a good indicator of the value you are creating for the customer. Strong pull equals high value.

Of course, there are exceptions. Sometimes there is a little underlying "problem" being solved by a wildly successful product or service. Take the Pet Rock. More than 1 million Pet Rocks were sold in the mid-1970s, despite being just what it sounds like—a rock that was sold as a pet. Although this example flies in the face of the concept that the best ideas have to solve large problems, the exceptions to this rule are few in number, and we maintain that solving small problems is still a losing strategy for creating valuable ventures.

ARE YOU LOSING SLEEP OVER YOUR IDEA?

Passion is hard to mistake. Are you losing sleep because you can't stop thinking about your idea?[1] Are you talking to all of your friends about it? Are they excited, too? Analyzing your level of passion and enthusiasm is important when evaluating an idea, not only because you're using yourself as a stand-in barometer for your future customers (if you don't like it, why would they?), but also because successfully launching a venture can take years of your life. Most people are not willing to make such a sacrifice for an idea about which they are lukewarm. To see a venture through, and to make the investment in time, money, and life for it to succeed, you have to be in love with the idea.

DO YOU HAVE A LEG UP (OR MAYBE TWO LEGS) OVER YOUR COMPETITION?

A *competitive advantage* is anything that gives you a proverbial "leg up" over your competition, including high product quality, level of service, degree of customization, usability of technology, support of online influencers, product knowledge or expertise, low price, faster production, and cheaper delivery, just to name a few. All the better if your competition is "boxed out" from actually competing with you.

Choosing ideas that exhibit these elements, or the potential for them, is important, and you can narrow your lists down by choosing ideas that offer goods or services to your customers that are unique, valuable, and hard to imitate or copy. If your idea can easily be copied by competitors, then you have what is called a "low barrier to entry," and these kinds of ideas or products lead to very short-term competitive advantage, if any at all.

When evaluating your ideas, you may modify them slightly in order to provide a greater competitive advantage. You can do this by moving from a "commodity" to some offering that is differentiated from the competition or the substitute good, which then increases its value in the eyes of the customer while underscoring its perceived uniqueness.

You may also be able to create some sort of barrier to entry to minimize competition. Barriers to entry are commonly some form of intellectual property, such as patents. If the venture uses some creation (invention) that is novel, useful, and not obvious, it may qualify for a patent (in the United States, at least). Because a patent gives an inventor an amount of time in which to sell the product without direct competition, it can provide an incredible advantage.

Barriers need not always be patents, however. Entrepreneurs have created barriers in many creative ways. Remember Soft Soap? By buying up all pumps available from suppliers, they were able to create a barrier to entry for powerhouse competitors such as Johnson & Johnson and Procter & Gamble. This strategy bought them about a six-month head start on the competition—enough of a barrier to establish customer loyalty and shed some of the fragility that plagues early-stage startups.

Barriers can also be created by relationships with suppliers or customers, through contract, or by a special skill or ability that others can't easily obtain or replicate.

IS YOUR SOLUTION PROFITABLE?

Profit potential can be determined primarily from three main components of your solution: the size of the market you're selling into, your solution's margin, and how price-sensitive your customers are.

Profit potential can also be viewed as "impact potential" for nonprofit startups. For a nonprofit venture to be sustainable, the impact created must be demonstrated in order to continue to find resources, in the form of either donors or income generated through activities. Whether for-profit or nonprofit, the three-step evaluation process that is introduced below still applies.

CAN YOU TAKE *YOU* OUT OF YOUR IDEA?

Entrepreneurs struggle with all sorts of cognitive biases. In other words, we are often not objective about our ideas; entrepreneurs often love their ideas much more than the market does! One of the key biases is confirmation bias. Simply put, entrepreneurs hear only what they want to hear. They talk to customers, or otherwise research customers, and look for information that confirms their idea and sometimes dismiss feedback that does not confirm their idea. This doesn't really make sense if you think about it because the entrepreneur has the most to lose if the idea does not make it successfully to market. Although it is important to be passionate and to believe in your ideas, it is equally important to listen objectively to what the market has to say. Is there really evidence that a market would support your idea? By learning to evaluate your ideas objectively, you put yourself in the best position to make a good decision about whether or not to invest more of your valuable time, energy, and resources in executing the idea.

CHOOSING YOUR TOP 10 OF 50 IDEAS

Before moving on, it's important that you have scored each batch of 10 ideas from the Identify, Discover, Enhance, Anticipate, and Target chapters. From those scores, now take your top 10 ideas—those with the highest scores among the 50. Record that batch of 10 below, or on a spreadsheet, index cards, or simply a plain sheet of paper.

Rank	Score	Idea
1		
2		
3		
4		
5		
6		
7		
8		
9		
10		

TWO FOR THREE: A TWO-STEP EVALUATION PROCESS TO GET YOU TO YOUR STRONGEST THREE IDEAS

Now we are going to help you evaluate your 10 best ideas so that you can identify the top three with the strongest potential! The Evaluation process introduced here is not the same scoring mechanism as the one used on the other 50 ideas. Instead, it is two-step process designed to help evaluate which of the top 10 ideas most deserve to be the final top three:

- Step 1: Google search

- Step 2: IDEATE evaluation

Step 1: Google Search

Using a simple term search on Google, research each of your 10 ideas. For example, if your idea is the dog hair catch for a drain (mentioned in Chapter 2), you might search Google for "dog hair drain guard" in order to see what comes up. The results can reveal what other solutions exist in the marketplace. It's likely that your idea will come up in this simple Google search. If it does, you have two choices: You can feel dejected and demoralized because the idea you love already exists, or you can feel elated because this is evidence of early market validation. Go with the latter if you can determine whether you can create differentiation between your idea and what's showing up on Google. Now, if your Google search turns up nothing, you must discover how potential customers are currently solving their problems. If customers are doing nothing to solve the problem, this may indicate that the problem is not severe enough to solve.

No "score" is attached to this activity, but the results may rule out an idea or propel it to the top of the list. If an idea search shows numerous competitors are doing almost the same thing, that idea should likely fall off the list. If an idea has few competitors but a lot of content regarding the need for a solution (through forums or social networks), that idea should rise.

Step 2: IDEATE Evaluation

Next, score each of your top 10 ideas (from 1 to 5) for each of the six sections (I-D-E-A-T-E). The sum of those scores will give you your final, total score to use to rank your top 10 ideas.

This isn't meant to be a strict, scientific process at this point, but rather a quick method to help you cull from the plethora of possibilities. Here are some questions you can ask to arrive at your scores:

How large is the migraine headache problem?

Are you addressing the root cause of the migraine headache problem, and is your solution meaningful to it?

Are people willing to pay for your solution?

Is this an area of passion for you?

Can you leverage your knowledge, network, or other assets?

Was the idea found in a problem-rich environment?

Does the solution capitalize on current trends that may lead to a new market?

Is this an evolutionary leap over what exists currently?

Is there an opportunity to expand on this idea to make it grow past what it is now?

Are you building value for all stakeholders (beyond the customer)?

Does the idea take into account anticipated social, demographic, technological, political, regulatory, or industry changes?

Is the idea forward-looking and part of a growing market as opposed to a stagnant market?

Is the solution one that is likely to have a lot competitors once the underlying problem is identified?

Do you know who the buyer is?

Is the buyer an attractive customer (has money, has purchasing power, isn't price sensitive, needs your item)?

Is the solution meeting specific and confirmed customer needs?

Are you solving a problem with a "pull" solution?

Are you losing sleep over your idea? (Note: "Yes" is a good thing!)

Is the idea unique and difficult for others to imitate?

Is there a clear path to earning revenue and creating a profitable venture?

Idea	I	D	E	A	T	E	Total Score
Idea	I	D	E	A	T	E	Total Score
Idea	I	D	E	A	T	E	Total Score
Idea	I	D	E	A	T	E	Total Score
Idea	I	D	E	A	T	E	Total Score
Idea	I	D	E	A	T	E	Total Score
Idea	I	D	E	A	T	E	Total Score
Idea	I	D	E	A	T	E	Total Score
Idea	I	D	E	A	T	E	Total Score
Idea	I	D	E	A	T	E	Total Score

CONCEPT STATEMENTS FOR YOUR TOP THREE IDEAS

Now that you have three solid ideas, it's time to put pen to paper and clearly articulate what these three ideas are. A useful tool is a concept statement, which is a brief description of your idea. In one to two sentences, describe what your idea is, the problem it solves, and for whom. For example, it is a useful exercise to fill in the following blanks:

_____[Idea] is _____[description] for _____ [target market] that _____[problem it solves].[2]

For example, *SnappyScreen is a height adjustable, fully autonomous, touchless sunscreen application machine for customers of beach hotels/resorts that applies the perfect amount of sunscreen so that people can spend less time stressing over sunscreen and more time enjoying fun in the sun.*

Your concept statement should offer a brief, yet clear description of the idea, the target market, and the value generated or problem being solved for the customer. In the boxes below, write concept statements for your top three ideas.

Concept 1

Concept 2

Concept 3

SELF-REFLECTION ON EVALUATION

Think about the process used to get from 10 to 3 ideas.

- How did you feel moving from 10 to 3 ideas?

_____

_____

_____

_____

_____

_____

_____

_____

_____

_____

- Did the process help you identify more valuable ideas? In what way?

_____

_____

_____

_____

_____

_____

_____

_____

_____

_____

- What are the top three lessons you will not forget about the IDEATE method?

_____

_____

_____

_____

_____

_____

_____

_____

_____

_____

8

IDEATE 50 MORE

In order to develop a few really strong ideas, it is important to be prolific. Linus Pauling, winner of the both the Nobel Peace Prize and the Nobel Prize in Chemistry, said, "The best way to have a good idea is to have lots of ideas." The best ideas come from students who have multiple high-quality ideas from which to choose. It is extremely rare that a student has one really strong idea in a small pool of poor-quality ideas.

100 IDEAS IS NOT A "NICE TO HAVE"— IT'S A "NEED TO HAVE"

You have generated 50 ideas so far, but we still need to get to 100 ideas—the minimum likely needed to generate a valuable idea. Feel free to go beyond 100. And don't think of this as a one-time assignment. If you are interested in becoming an entrepreneur, this is a process you should go through continuously.

As you develop your next set of 50 ideas, consider all the lessons you have learned so far:

- Identify a migraine headache problem and develop a solution to resolve it.

- Make sure a lot of people have the same headache.

- Ensure that people are willing to pay for a solution.

- Find customers already spending money on inferior solutions and create a superior solution.

- Identify root causes of problems, not just surface-level problems.

- Don't shy away from ideas that already exist because you have built-in market validation.

- Stay away from small niche markets.

- If you can't find a customer, then you don't have a valuable solution.

- If you can't articulate the value proposition to customers (or anyone), then there is no value.

- Avoid markets that have low barriers to competition.

- Bring something into a market that cannot be easily obtained elsewhere.

- Use your own expertise and talent to search for problems that others haven't yet spotted.

- Understand that new opportunities can come from problems you encounter, but don't be your only customer!

- Examine your passions to discover even more opportunities.

- Bring experiences back from other places and see whether they can work in your "place."

- Look at changes in society, technology, industry, and government and anticipate opportunities that are likely to emerge.

- Add something new to existing ideas for enhancement.

- Reimagine something old into something new by adding technology.

- Build value not only for your customer but for everyone else connected to the idea.

- Look for entrepreneurs who have enhancement-based startups because their enhancement may lead to changes that you can capitalize on with your own enhancements.

- Understand your target market and its needs and wants.

- Don't start with a solution: Start with target customers and create something for them.

- Talk to target customers and learn more about them.

- Most important, make sure you are extremely enthusiastic about solving the headache problems that you identify. That enthusiasm will give you needed energy on the good days and bad.

YOU KNOW WHAT TO DO NOW, SO APPLY YOUR LEARNING

Now that you've completed the IDEATE framework once, you should have the confidence to move around the different parts of the framework as you wish, rather than going through it sequentially. This is why we are asking you to generate 50 ideas however you want, rather than forcing you to generate batches of 10 ideas. However, feel free to follow the framework using batches of 10 ideas. We do think it's easier to focus on batches of 10. Plus, your brain needs time to rest and recover!

Just don't fall in love too soon with your early ideas and stop IDEATE-ing. Of course, take pride in your creativity, intelligence, and hard work but not at the expense of other, perhaps even better ideas. Often, our earliest ideas are common ones that others have also identified, making them the least valuable. Digging deeper, really studying the problem, understanding root causes, generating many ideas to solve a problem, combining ideas, enhancing ideas—this is why so many ideas are needed to get at a high-potential opportunity. This is why you need to come up with another 50 ideas!

READY. SET. IDEATE.

The charts that follow should look very familiar to you by now. You know what to do.

1. Record the problem and associated idea.

2. (MHP × Enthusiasm) + Gut = Total Score

3. Rank your 50 ideas so you can take your 10 strongest ideas forward for evaluation.

4. Apply the Google test to the top 10. Remove those ideas that don't pass.

5. Apply the IDEATE evaluation to the remaining ideas (10 or fewer ideas).

6. Identify the ideas with the top three scores.

7. Write a concept statement for each of your top three ideas.

Problem identified:			Rank (1–10)
Idea description:			Score
MHP (1–5):	Enthusiasm (1–5):	Gut (1–5):	Total ([MHP × E] + G):

Problem identified:			Rank (1–10)
Idea description:			Score
MHP (1–5):	Enthusiasm (1–5):	Gut (1–5):	Total ([MHP × E] + G):

Problem identified:			Rank (1–10)
Idea description:			Score
MHP (1–5):	Enthusiasm (1–5):	Gut (1–5):	Total ([MHP × E] + G):

Problem identified:			**Rank (1–10)**
Idea description:			**Score**
MHP (1–5):	Enthusiasm (1–5):	Gut (1–5):	Total ([MHP × E] + G):

Problem identified:			**Rank (1–10)**
Idea description:			**Score**
MHP (1–5):	Enthusiasm (1–5):	Gut (1–5):	Total ([MHP × E] + G):

Problem identified:			**Rank (1–10)**
Idea description:			**Score**
MHP (1–5):	Enthusiasm (1–5):	Gut (1–5):	Total ([MHP × E] + G):

Problem identified:			**Rank (1–10)**
Idea description:			**Score**
MHP (1–5):	Enthusiasm (1–5):	Gut (1–5):	Total ([MHP × E] + G):

Problem identified:	**Rank (1–10)**
Idea description:	**Score**

MHP (1–5):	Enthusiasm (1–5):	Gut (1–5):	Total ([MHP × E] + G):

Problem identified:	**Rank (1–10)**
Idea description:	**Score**

MHP (1–5):	Enthusiasm (1–5):	Gut (1–5):	Total ([MHP × E] + G):

Problem identified:	**Rank (1–10)**
Idea description:	**Score**

MHP (1–5):	Enthusiasm (1–5):	Gut (1–5):	Total ([MHP × E] + G):

Problem identified:	**Rank (1–10)**
Idea description:	**Score**

MHP (1–5):	Enthusiasm (1–5):	Gut (1–5):	Total ([MHP × E] + G):

Problem identified:			Rank (1–10)
Idea description:			Score
MHP (1–5):	Enthusiasm (1–5):	Gut (1–5):	Total ([MHP × E] + G):

Problem identified:			Rank (1–10)
Idea description:			Score
MHP (1–5):	Enthusiasm (1–5):	Gut (1–5):	Total ([MHP × E] + G):

Problem identified:			Rank (1–10)
Idea description:			Score
MHP (1–5):	Enthusiasm (1–5):	Gut (1–5):	Total ([MHP × E] + G):

Problem identified:			Rank (1–10)
Idea description:			Score
MHP (1–5):	Enthusiasm (1–5):	Gut (1–5):	Total ([MHP × E] + G):

Problem identified:			**Rank (1–10)**
Idea description:			**Score**
MHP (1–5):	Enthusiasm (1–5):	Gut (1–5):	Total ([MHP × E] + G):

Problem identified:			**Rank (1–10)**
Idea description:			**Score**
MHP (1–5):	Enthusiasm (1–5):	Gut (1–5):	Total ([MHP × E] + G):

Problem identified:			**Rank (1–10)**
Idea description:			**Score**
MHP (1–5):	Enthusiasm (1–5):	Gut (1–5):	Total ([MHP × E] + G):

Problem identified:			**Rank (1–10)**
Idea description:			**Score**
MHP (1–5):	Enthusiasm (1–5):	Gut (1–5):	Total ([MHP × E] + G):

Problem identified:			**Rank (1–10)**
Idea description:			**Score**
MHP (1–5):	Enthusiasm (1–5):	Gut (1–5):	Total ([MHP × E] + G):

Problem identified:			**Rank (1–10)**
Idea description:			**Score**
MHP (1–5):	Enthusiasm (1–5):	Gut (1–5):	Total ([MHP × E] + G):

Problem identified:			**Rank (1–10)**
Idea description:			**Score**
MHP (1–5):	Enthusiasm (1–5):	Gut (1–5):	Total ([MHP × E] + G):

Problem identified:			**Rank (1–10)**
Idea description:			**Score**
MHP (1–5):	Enthusiasm (1–5):	Gut (1–5):	Total ([MHP × E] + G):

| Problem identified: | **Rank (1–10)** |
| Idea description: | **Score** |

| MHP (1–5): | Enthusiasm (1–5): | Gut (1–5): | Total ([MHP × E] + G): |

| Problem identified: | **Rank (1–10)** |
| Idea description: | **Score** |

| MHP (1–5): | Enthusiasm (1–5): | Gut (1–5): | Total ([MHP × E] + G): |

| Problem identified: | **Rank (1–10)** |
| Idea description: | **Score** |

| MHP (1–5): | Enthusiasm (1–5): | Gut (1–5): | Total ([MHP × E] + G): |

| Problem identified: | **Rank (1–10)** |
| Idea description: | **Score** |

| MHP (1–5): | Enthusiasm (1–5): | Gut (1–5): | Total ([MHP × E] + G): |

Problem identified:			**Rank (1–10)**
Idea description:			**Score**
MHP (1–5):	Enthusiasm (1–5):	Gut (1–5):	Total ([MHP × E] + G):

Problem identified:			**Rank (1–10)**
Idea description:			**Score**
MHP (1–5):	Enthusiasm (1–5):	Gut (1–5):	Total ([MHP × E] + G):

Problem identified:			**Rank (1–10)**
Idea description:			**Score**
MHP (1–5):	Enthusiasm (1–5):	Gut (1–5):	Total ([MHP × E] + G):

Problem identified:			**Rank (1–10)**
Idea description:			**Score**
MHP (1–5):	Enthusiasm (1–5):	Gut (1–5):	Total ([MHP × E] + G):

Problem identified:			**Rank (1–10)**
Idea description:			**Score**
MHP (1–5):	Enthusiasm (1–5):	Gut (1–5):	Total ([MHP × E] + G):

Problem identified:			**Rank (1–10)**
Idea description:			**Score**
MHP (1–5):	Enthusiasm (1–5):	Gut (1–5):	Total ([MHP × E] + G):

Problem identified:			**Rank (1–10)**
Idea description:			**Score**
MHP (1–5):	Enthusiasm (1–5):	Gut (1–5):	Total ([MHP × E] + G):

Problem identified:			**Rank (1–10)**
Idea description:			**Score**
MHP (1–5):	Enthusiasm (1–5):	Gut (1–5):	Total ([MHP × E] + G):

Problem identified:			Rank (1–10)
Idea description:			Score
MHP (1–5):	Enthusiasm (1–5):	Gut (1–5):	Total ([MHP × E] + G):

Problem identified:			Rank (1–10)
Idea description:			Score
MHP (1–5):	Enthusiasm (1–5):	Gut (1–5):	Total ([MHP × E] + G):

Problem identified:			Rank (1–10)
Idea description:			Score
MHP (1–5):	Enthusiasm (1–5):	Gut (1–5):	Total ([MHP × E] + G):

Problem identified:			Rank (1–10)
Idea description:			Score
MHP (1–5):	Enthusiasm (1–5):	Gut (1–5):	Total ([MHP × E] + G):

Problem identified:	Rank (1–10)
Idea description:	**Score**

MHP (1–5):	Enthusiasm (1–5):	Gut (1–5):	Total ([MHP × E] + G):

Problem identified:	Rank (1–10)
Idea description:	**Score**

MHP (1–5):	Enthusiasm (1–5):	Gut (1–5):	Total ([MHP × E] + G):

Problem identified:	Rank (1–10)
Idea description:	**Score**

MHP (1–5):	Enthusiasm (1–5):	Gut (1–5):	Total ([MHP × E] + G):

Problem identified:	Rank (1–10)
Idea description:	**Score**

MHP (1–5):	Enthusiasm (1–5):	Gut (1–5):	Total ([MHP × E] + G):

Problem identified:			Rank (1–10)
Idea description:			Score
MHP (1–5):	Enthusiasm (1–5):	Gut (1–5):	Total ([MHP × E] + G):

Problem identified:			Rank (1–10)
Idea description:			Score
MHP (1–5):	Enthusiasm (1–5):	Gut (1–5):	Total ([MHP × E] + G):

Problem identified:			Rank (1–10)
Idea description:			Score
MHP (1–5):	Enthusiasm (1–5):	Gut (1–5):	Total ([MHP × E] + G):

Problem identified:			Rank (1–10)
Idea description:			Score
MHP (1–5):	Enthusiasm (1–5):	Gut (1–5):	Total ([MHP × E] + G):

Problem identified:	Rank (1–10)
Idea description:	Score
MHP (1–5):	Enthusiasm (1–5):	Gut (1–5):	Total ([MHP × E] + G):

Problem identified:	Rank (1–10)
Idea description:	Score
MHP (1–5):	Enthusiasm (1–5):	Gut (1–5):	Total ([MHP × E] + G):

Problem identified:	Rank (1–10)
Idea description:	Score
MHP (1–5):	Enthusiasm (1–5):	Gut (1–5):	Total ([MHP × E] + G):

CHOOSING YOUR TOP 10 OF 50 IDEAS

Now take your top 10 ideas—those with the highest scores among the 50. Record that batch of 10 below, on a spreadsheet, index cards, or simply a plain sheet of paper.

Rank	Score	Idea
1		
2		
3		
4		
5		
6		
7		
8		
9		
10		

TWO FOR THREE: IT'S TIME TO EVALUATE AGAIN

Now it's time to evaluate your 10 best ideas from your new batch of 50 so that you can identify the top three with the strongest potential! The Evaluation process is the same process introduced in Chapter 7:

- Step 1: Conduct a Google search to determine whether the solution or similar solutions exist.

- Step 2: Review the questions in Chapter 7 in the section "Step 2: IDEATE Evaluation." Then, evaluate your chosen 10 ideas using the table below.

Idea	I	D	E	A	T	E	Total Score
Idea	I	D	E	A	T	E	Total Score
Idea	I	D	E	A	T	E	Total Score
Idea	I	D	E	A	T	E	Total Score
Idea	I	D	E	A	T	E	Total Score

Idea	I	D	E	A	T	E	Total Score

Idea	I	D	E	A	T	E	Total Score

Idea	I	D	E	A	T	E	Total Score

Idea	I	D	E	A	T	E	Total Score

Idea	I	D	E	A	T	E	Total Score

CONCEPT STATEMENTS FOR YOUR TOP THREE IDEAS

Next, write concept statements for your three highest ranked ideas. If you need a how-to refresher, refer to Chapter 7.

Concept Statement 1

Concept Statement 2

Concept Statement 3

SELF-REFLECTION ON IDEATE-ING 50 MORE

- Was it more or less difficult to generate a second batch of 50 ideas? Why?

_____

_____

_____

_____

_____

_____

_____

_____

_____

- Do you recognize any patterns in how you spot new ideas? For example, do you tend to identify, discover, anticipate, or enhance to generate new ideas? Or, do you apply the different approaches equally?

_____

_____

_____

_____

_____

_____

_____

_____

_____

- What parts of the IDEATE method did you feel were practiced most often as you generated this second batch of 50 ideas?

_____

_____

_____

_____

_____

_____

_____

_____

CHOOSE ONE BIG, VALUABLE, IMPACTFUL, FEASIBLE, AND PROFITABLE IDEA

You've done a ton of work if you are reading this chapter. Congratulations! At this time, we expect that you've generated 100 ideas and you have analyzed and evaluated those ideas to the point where you have six solid ideas—3 from the first batch of 50 and 3 from the second batch of 50. Now it's time to decide which idea you want to pursue and further test its viability as a new venture.

ENTREPRENEURSHIP IS REALLY A GAME OF GUTS AND ESTIMATES!

Entrepreneurs do their best to analyze opportunities, collect the most important data, and answer the critical questions, but there are no sure bets. Throughout this workbook, we've asked you to score and rank your ideas, but your scores are estimates. They are guesses based on what you know, the research you've done, the actions taken, and even a gut feel and enthusiasm level. The scores in the previous chapters are meant to be guides and signals rather than verifiable scientific data. Yet the numbers help you. They help you compare one idea against another, and this is important when you are comparing 100 ideas. But, now you are down to six ideas. It's time to stop scoring and do some final "checks" on your final six ideas. These checks will help you narrow your six ideas down to one. We know it may be hard to get to one idea. It's common for entrepreneurs to play with two or three ideas at the same time in the early stages. But, in order to complete this workbook, we expect you to complete an Idea Board for at least one idea. However, you may actually need to complete two or three Idea Boards. Before we get to the Idea Board, let's talk about three different "checks."

RISK CHECK TO SEE WHETHER IT CAN BE DONE

There are two primary types of "risk" that entrepreneurs (and investors) evaluate when looking at new ideas: execution risk and invention risk. If the idea definitely can be done (e.g., that pancake pillow mentioned in Chapter 3), then there is no invention risk behind the idea, only execution risk, which describes your ability to create a brand and a product that people want to buy.

If, on the other hand, there exists only a possibility of your idea ever actually working—whether because the technology doesn't yet exist to make it possible or affordable or because it's just impossible (the dream of a perpetual motion machine)—then that is invention risk. Invention risk is common in the field of pharmaceuticals; the drugs being developed today may never see the light of day, even if the research and development team has the best plan in the world to commercialize them. Ideas with high invention risk are harder to manage, typically take longer for a business to reach scale, and have serious barriers to entry in order to be feasible. Generally speaking, ideas that have invention risk should be ranked slightly lower than those with only execution risk, unless you have special skills or knowledge in the field to overcome the invention risk.

Evaluate your top six ideas to see if any of them have invention risk. Absent a competitive advantage to overcome that risk, it's likely that those ideas will fall lower on your list.

The risk check question is "Can I get the resources I need to execute the idea?"

VALUE CHECK TO ENSURE IT'S GOOD FOR ALL

High-quality ideas are good for all or they are good for none. Ideas must create value for entrepreneurs, their customers, and any other stakeholders in their network (suppliers, service providers, etc.). This concept is referred to as the "three-legged stool," discussed in Chapter 4; if one of the three legs of the stool is removed, the entire stool will fall, just as a business will fail if all participants in the creation, running, and consumption of the business and its products don't benefit. Refer to Chapter 4 for a refresher on this topic, in order to help reduce your top six ideas to one.

Here is an example of a sturdy three-legged stool to help you when narrowing down your top ideas. SnappyScreen, the previously mentioned sunscreen application machine, has a sturdy three-legged stool. It creates value for all. It creates value for parents because children often hate the traditional sunscreen application process and often fight it vigorously. That is stressful for parents who are trying to de-stress while on vacation. Children actually enjoy having sunscreen applied in the SnappyScreen machine because they get to spin 360 degrees while the machine quickly coats them in sunscreen. So it is fun rather than tedious and children want to do it. It is very quick—you can sunscreen a family of four in a minute or two—so families can spend more time on fun activities. SnappyScreen creates value for the hotel because sunburned guests spend less money while at the hotel and are more likely to write a negative review, according to SnappyScreen founders. Finally, as SnappyScreen grows and helps more people protect their skin and enjoy their vacations more, it will generate economies of scale and profitable operations, thus making SnappyScreen viable long term by creating value for the founders. Of course, it also creates value for all suppliers, such as those that produce the component parts of the SnappyScreen application machine and all of the ingredients that go into the sunscreen. So, everyone that is involved with SnappyScreen wins—it is truly "good for all." Now, think through your top ideas in a similar fashion. Remember to be aware of confirmation bias and to look at your ideas with an objective lens. Are your ideas good for all involved? If not, can you enhance the idea in some way? If no, they may fall lower on your list.

The value check question is "Is the idea good for customers, me (the entrepreneur), and stakeholders?"

GUT CHECK FOR SANITY

Evaluation tools are certainly important, but not everything can be reduced to a rubric or score. This is not an exact science. Great entrepreneurs are said to live comfortably in the future. They see things that other people simply miss. This is known as vision or gut instinct. When this vision is communicated to others who do not get it, they may react negatively toward the idea. If you see something clearly and truly believe in it, pay heed to that feeling. If you are passionate about it and your belief is strong, pay attention to that feeling. Trust your gut instinct. If your gut is screaming no, remove the idea from your list.

The gut check question is "Is the idea really worth pursuing?"

THE IDEA BOARD

Okay, we have reached the point where you need to create one final deliverable. By now you have taken your top six ideas through a risk check, value check, and gut check. What did you learn? Which idea emerged at the top of the list? Now it's time to choose your best idea and create an Idea Board using the template shown in Table 9.1.

Table 9.1 Idea Board			
NAME *Just create something!* **TAGLINE** *What's the snappy, one-sentence description?*	**CONCEPT STATEMENT** *1-2 sentences that describe the idea, the problem it solves, and for whom.*		
MIGRAINE HEADACHE SIZE *What's the problem and how big is it?* *What are people doing to currently solve the problem?*	**COMPELLING VISUAL** *What does it look like? Show the idea in action.*		
UNIQUENESS *How does it go beyond what is currently being done?* **TARGET CUSTOMER** *Describe your ideal customer.*	**RESOURCES AT HAND** *What do you have that you can use to take immediate, early action? (people, financial, informational, technological)*	**VALUE GENERATED** *What's in it for the customer? What's in it for stakeholders? What's in it for me, the entrepreneur?*	**HAPPY METER** ☺ *Level of enthusiasm about the idea!* 1 2 low 3 4 5 6 7 8 9 10 high *circle one*

Source: Idea Board is based on a version created by and used with permission from Heidi Neck, Babson College.

100 IDEAS LATER

You did it! You created 100 ideas! If you are reading this and have done the work, we hope you have at least one big, valuable, impactful, feasible, and profitable idea. You may not know what you have for sure at this very moment, but you've done enough work to move to the next steps with your Idea Board. Where do you start? Share your Idea Board with as many people as possible: potential customers, suppliers, friends, mentors, professors, and other trusted advisors. Because we love the boldness of the number 100, we suggest you talk to 100 people. Listen to every person you talk to and record notes during and after each conversation. If you don't know 100 people (which is likely), then ask every person you consult to recommend someone else you should approach. Your idea will be influenced and improved by every conversation. As well, your network will expand in the process and you will grow as a future entrepreneur.

NOTES

Chapter 1

1. Idea generation and opportunity identification has a longstanding history and place in the field of entrepreneurship. The following represents selected seminal works on the topic: Baron, R. A., & Henry, R. A. (2010). How entrepreneurs acquire the capacity to excel: Insights from research on expert performance. *Strategic Entrepreneurship Journal, 4*(1), 49–65; Corbett, A. C. (2005). Experiential learning within the process of opportunity identification and exploitation. *Entrepreneurship Theory and Practice, 29*(4), 473–491; DeTienne, D. R., & Chandler, G. N. (2004). Opportunity identification and its role in the entrepreneurial classroom: A pedagogical approach and empirical test. *Academy of management learning & education, 3*(3), 242–257; Gaglio, C. M., & Katz, J. A. (2001). The psychological basis of opportunity identification: Entrepreneurial alertness. *Small Business Economics, 16*(2), 95–111; Haynie, J. M., Shepherd, D., Mosakowski, E., & Earley, P. C. (2010). A situated metacognitive model of the entrepreneurial mindset. *Journal of Business Venturing, 25*(2), 217–229; Shepherd, D. A., & DeTienne, D. R. (2005). Prior knowledge, potential financial reward, and opportunity identification. *Entrepreneurship Theory and Practice, 29*(1), 91–112.

2. Baron, R. A., & Ensley, M. D. (2006). Opportunity recognition as the detection of meaningful patterns: Evidence from comparisons of novice and experienced entrepreneurs. *Management Science, 52*(9), 1331–1344.

3. Cohen, D., Shinnar, R.S., & Hsu, D. K. (2019). *Enhancing opportunity recognition skills in entrepreneurship education: A new approach and empirical test.* 2019 Babson College Entrepreneurship Research Conference, Babson Park, MA.

4. Please contact the authors if you would like to receive a copy of the academic paper.

5. Shane, S. A. (2004). *Finding fertile ground: Identifying extraordinary opportunities for new business.* New York, NY: Wharton Business School.

Chapter 2

1. Baron, R. A., & Ensley, M. D. (2006). Opportunity recognition as the detection of meaningful patterns: Evidence from comparisons of novice and experienced entrepreneurs. *Management Science, 52*(9), 1331–1344.

2. Shane, S. A. (2004). *Finding fertile ground: Identifying extraordinary opportunities for new business.* New York, NY: Wharton Business School.

Chapter 3

1. Fiet, J. (2002). *The systematic search for entrepreneurial discoveries.* Westport, CT: Quorum Books.

Chapter 5

1. Shane, S. A. (2004). *Finding fertile ground: Identifying extraordinary opportunities for new business.* New York, NY: Wharton Business School.

2. Baron, R. A., & Ensley, M. D. (2006). Opportunity recognition as the detection of meaningful patterns: Evidence from comparisons of novice and experienced entrepreneurs. *Management Science, 52*(9), 1331–1344.

3. Cilluffo, A., & Cohn, D. (2018, April 15). 7 demographic trends shaping the U.S. and the world in 2018. *Pew Research Center.* Retrieved from https://www.pewresearch.org/fact-tank/2018/04/25/7-demographic-trends-shaping-the-u-s-and-the-world-in-2018/

4. Calvo, D. (2019, February). The ride-hailing war: Uber's fight with taxis in Europe. *Androidpit.* Retrieved from https://www.androidpit.com/taxi-vs-uber-europe

5. Sheetz, M. (2017, August 24). Technology killing off corporate America: Average life span of companies under 20 years. *CNBC.* Retrieved from https://www.cnbc.com/2017/08/24/technology-killing-off-corporations-average-lifespan-of-company-under-20-years.html

6. Hsu, T. (2019, March 6). The world's last Blockbuster has no plans to close. *New York Times.* Retrieved from https://www.nytimes.com/2019/03/06/business/last-blockbuster-store.html

Chapter 7

1. Cohen, D., Cardon, M., & Singh, J. (2019). *A developmental framework for anticipatory entrepreneurial passion and its consequences for affect and effort for nascent entrepreneurs.* Paper accepted to Annual Proceedings of Academy of Management.

2. Format for concept statement from Neck, H., Neck, C., & Murray, E. (in press). *Entrepreneurship: The practice and mindset* (2nd ed.). Thousand Oaks, CA: SAGE.